ADVE[ ]

in the

SLOW LANE

-Tales From the Other Side-

Cherie
May the "Schwartz" be with you!

GARY SCHWARTZ

Gary Schwartz 2/00

HARD SHELL
PUBLISHING

Mukilteo, Washington

Publishers Note: Many of the products and services mentioned in these pieces are trademarks of their respective companies. Every effort was made to identify these trademarks by initial capitalization. Should there be an omission in this respect, we shall be pleased to make the necessary changes in future printings.

A Hardshell Publishing Book
PO BOX 1630 Mukilteo, WA 98275
Copyright © 1996 by Gary Schwartz

Library of Congress Catalog Card Number: 95-81678

ISBN: 0-9649558-2-2

Printed in the U.S.A.

10 9 8 7 6 5 4 3

Second Printing

TABLE OF FABLES

Dedication — Acknowledgments — Introduction

PART ONE: *Nonsense, Just for the Fun of It*

(continued)

PART TWO: *Anecdotes of the Human Condition*

PART THREE: *Life Is Politics;*
I'm No Politician

PART FOUR: *Mirror, Mirror, Off-the-Wall;*
Who Am I Anyway?

(continued)

PART FIVE: *If History Repeats Itself, Why Can We Stop It?*

PART SIX: *Seriously, Folks*

Dedication

Debbie, David and ***Diann***. Your inspiration, loyalty, tolerance and friendship have made my life worthwhile. ***Chaz*** and ***Dina***, you are not forgotten.

Ed Hess. You provided the opportunity and encouragement to begin this long journey.

Cardiologist ***Jeff Rose*** and surgeon ***Frank Nieto***. You kept my heart ticking so I could finish living.

Mom, ***Dad***. You died before you knew me, but . . .

"Yo parents, I did it!"

Acknowledgments

Thank you *David* for your brilliant and brutal editing. Sometimes I hated what you did to make my work better; and now that we're finished, I don't like what you did any better.

Thank you *Dr. Nancy Brainard* for your grammar and punctuation expertise. I didn't use it all because you don't like what I write, but you're still my good friend. And thank you *Richard Brainard* for the soothing piano recordings you so well selected for the dreaded hours needed to edit this symphony of words.

Thank you *Debbie* and *Rain* for your love and support — and especially your courage to tolerate my frequent tantrums.

Thank you *Paul* for providing editorial space in the *Beacon*. Because of you I'm infamous in Mukilteo — but more significant, I'm proud to call you my friend.

Thank yoo *Lars, Marlene* and *Marie* for your outstanding proof-reeding. I'm glad you kaught the missppellinng of my name in three places.

To all the strange and interesting people in the world, I thank you for the good things to write about.

And a very special thanks to all you newspaper editors and publishers across America who allow me to share my thoughts every week with the folks in your communities.

Introduction

I revere the wise tortoise. This wonderful creature symbolizes patience, tolerance and perseverance. His silent message rescued me from the frantic big-city life and carried me to *The Other Side,* where serenity provided the opportunity to find inner peace and write this book as well.

The tortoise wasn't *always* my role model. When I was younger I preferred the hare. I wanted to go through life in a blaze of glory, to win the race. I almost died from trying. I started my weekly column *Life in the Slow Lane* in 1987 while working in the business of public relations. It was the best escape therapy I could find; writing outrageous, yet hopefully humorous and meaningful thoughts about our lives. I made a feeble attempt at screenwriting, but once I discovered how the system worked, I realized I wasn't fit for the task — it was too much hard work.

I've always been considered a little different. I'm really not. But if I enjoy tormenting writing teachers with bizarre and unusual stories, don't like to get dressed everyday, don't think along the same lines as everybody else and shock strangers by asking them about their political views before saying "Hello," perhaps I should consider outside opinions.

I think humor is a necessary remedy for enduring the ills of life we all share. I use it frequently to soothe the indelible pain inflicted by the premature deaths of my parents.

Since we can't do much about our true nature, we should at least amuse ourselves by having fun interpreting it.

Humor and irreverence are good things. I hope you'll agree, and enjoy this book.

PART ONE:

Nonsense, Just For the Fun of It

"Hello, 911? We Need a Donut Shop"

The local police are feeling insecure. Who can blame them? The entire force is being considered for elimination to help balance the city budget.

What we need is a profitable donut shop. If I had the dough I'd open one. The increased tax revenue would help pay to keep the police here. Otherwise, we're in for a long, fast ride on the information superhighway — without anyone to give out tickets.

Can you imagine what could happen without a police force?

———————

"Honey, I can't sleep . . . the neighbor's dog again!"

"Call 911."

I reluctantly pushed the three buttons.

"You've reached the 911 emergency network. If you can't settle your family squabble in 20 minutes, call again and press 2 for a counselor. If this is a real emergency, press 1."

I pressed 1. "If you wish to speak to the dispatcher, take a chance and press 6. Your call will be answered in order by the day in which it was received. Otherwise, listen carefully."

I listened carefully. "Press 1 if there's a murder in progress . . . Press 11 if there's a burglary in progress . . . Press 14 if you're having a heart attack . . . Press 23 if you lost your lotto ticket, your pet or your mind . . . Press 31 if you can't find an open pizza parlor . . . Press 39 if you're too drunk to call in sick for work . . . Press 54 to report a stolen car . . . Press 69 if you need a companion . . . Press 87 for cocktails . . . Press your clothes if you're going to the Policeman's Charity Ball . . . Press 111 for barking dogs . . . Press . . ."

1

I pressed 111.

"You've reached the barking dog hotline. Press 1 for cocker spaniels . . . 2 for golden retrievers . . . 3 for bulldogs . . . 4 for poodles . . . 5 for Lassies . . . 6 for hot dogs . . ."

I slammed the phone down and ran out to the neighbor's yard. "Shut up." Buster barked louder. "Shut up, shut up!" My neighbor yelled out the window. "Shut up, shut up, shut up! I'm calling 911 to report you for disturbing the peace."

"Go for it."

Furious, I picked up a squirt gun and drove to the nearest bank. I waited in the dark for the first lone automated-teller customer. "This is a fake stick-up. Pretend I took your cash and stole your watch. Here's a quarter. Go to the phone booth. Call 911."

The startled guy laughed, but called anyway. "How much do you weigh? How much money are you robbing me for? What kind of watch are you taking?" We shrugged our shoulders in disbelief.

I sped 80 mph to the convenience store. "This is a stick-up." Feeling lucky, I asked for a gallon of ice cream and 900 lotto tickets. I gave the clerk my Social Security and driver's license numbers. "If you can't get through to the cops before I finish the ice cream or win the lotto, I'll do this again next month."

I raced 10 miles to the next town. At Donut Haven, I bought a dunker and took a seat among 14 of our neighboring city's finest. I dipped the donut in the ice cream but couldn't get it in my mouth. I had to take the ski mask off. The cops eyed me suspiciously.

"Any of you guys feel lucky?" I reached into the pocket of my camouflage jacket. "Got some good numbers here." I showed them my tickets. They weren't amused, but I got the attention I so desperately wanted.

I sped off, laying rubber in the parking lot to ensure I kept their interest. One of them took the bait. He followed me home.

He was about to handcuff and arrest me when Buster started in again. The cop, whose name was Bob, began checking my record on the car radio, but couldn't hear the response from headquarters. He gave Buster a stale donut to quiet him. Then he gave my neighbor — who began barking "no way, no way . . . " a $50 citation.

Bob and I went inside. "What's all the ruckus? Where were you?" asked my startled wife. "Nothing honey. Out looking for a cop. This is Bob. He took care of Buster."

We learned Bob had once worked here in town and wanted to come back. As he left he said, "You're right. A good cop is hard to find. I'll help you finance that donut shop."

A voice-mail 911 emergency system is a poor substitute for good cops and a good donut shop.

A town should know its priorities.

The Hoax of the Century — O.J. Gets the Lead

The O.J. Simpson trial was *really* a made-for-TV movie. It was the hoax of the century. The rubber bodies were planted by a Hollywood make-up artist doing authenticity testing for body doubles.

Those fascinating characters in the drama were *really* just wanna-be actors auditioning for larger roles in feature films. Most of them needed the exposure, although the honorable and contemplative Judge Ito has now returned to his meditations high atop the mountains of Tibet, without anymore objections.

Did you wonder why we *really* couldn't see members of the jury? They weren't important — just Hollywood casting directors, producers and screenwriters. If we knew that, we'd have known the trial was just a movie and we wouldn't have stayed tuned for the commercials when sidebars occurred. (*A sidebar is when the lawyers and judge get together for drinks during stressful scenes. A script supervisor, acting as the court reporter, helps them with their lines*).

O.J. and F. Lee Bailey were the only actors playing themselves. Because of their outstanding performances, O.J. signed a lucrative contract with the J&J Cutlery Company and Mr. Bailey is training with Barbara Walters to interview Mike Tyson, Don King and the Menendez brothers. O.J. did lose his Hertz contract, but his dizzying Bronco demo on the freeways earned him a gig with Ford.

Only in America!

A screenwriter friend of mine, helping with the new comedy sequel, *If the Glove Fits, Wear It*, gave me a copy of the script. I counted 120 uses of the *F* word, 95 uses of the *D* word and 186 of the *S* word. He said there were 200 *O* words (*objections*) from members of the panel to the use of any of them.

Here are some revealing excerpts from the casting meeting.

"Johnny was really good. He could sure do some talking. I think he'd be excellent as Jonnie, the senator accused of conspiracy. But we can't start shooting until he completes his evangelist tour."

"I think Barry could do very well in the part of the swinging, singing, loose-cannon detective. But I hear he needs to rest his voice for two months. He injured his cords yelling at the judge."

"Okay, we'll shoot around him."

"What about Marcia? Do you think she could pull it off as Linda, the former *Playboy* model accused of covering up? Her stint as the before-and-after model for that Beverly Hills salon certainly paid off. She looked great with those new hairdos and fancy suits. And what about her partner? Do you think he could play Stanley?"

"That's a tough one. Chris might not be able to remember his lines in that hot, sexy scene with Francine. He bombed during *the fuse is getting shorter* scene. He lost his place too many times."

"You're right. But I'm sure that blonde *Court TV* reporter wouldn't have any trouble playing Francine. She was terrific."

"She should be. She's not an actress."

"Oh."

"Now, that Fuhrman guy. Wow! Can you believe how well he played a Nazi think-alike. For a board member of the NAACP and the ACLU to pull that off, he deserves an Academy Award. What great screen presence and believability."

4

"Yep. And he also knows something about inner-city police work. He was arrested a long time ago."

"No kidding? What for?"

"He yelled obscenities at a cop during the Watts riots for arresting a friend of his who had looted a glove and shoe store. He's definitely got a part. He'll be a great straight man opposite Barry's singing cop."

"Well, I think we've got some pretty good prospects here. That witness, what's his name, who played the confused car detailer — boy was he good — although it's hard to believe a professor would risk his career for such a small part in a TV movie. I like his chutzpah. And the lady with the two watches? She's definitely in, too. She'll be perfect as the bimbo bookie at the race track. I hear in real life she was arrested for turning back auto odometers."

"Hey. Who's going to play Jimbo, the get-away driver?"

"That's easy. That innocent-looking guy who played the limo driver. He just got out of jail again for auto theft."

"What about Kato?"

"Forget him. He was terrible. Can't act worth a damn!"

"So how much do you think O.J. wants to play the lead?"

"We'll have to negotiate, but I think he'll be delighted to do his glove routine again. He sure enjoyed that scene, and he'll get to keep the gloves that fit."

I can't sit through another convoluted movie like this. Although I'm happy some of those characters will have gainful employment for a few months in a new feature film, it would be a shame to waste such talent on another made-for-TV movie.

But the biggest shame of all is the unnecessary loss of two *real* human beings. I wish it were *true* that Elvis was spotted in an up-scale Chicago bar, serving martinis to Ron and Nicole.

A Ray of Light From the Dark Side

I never believed there was life after death until now.

My thoughts will *always* be alive in this book. Hopefully, you'll think of them as good deeds. And being dead isn't really that bad, I can assure you. There's always light where there's dark and immortality for the deeds that are done.

Let me tell you how I know. After I died, I spent several weeks in Hell for orientation, then was sent here to Heaven for rest and recuperation.

Hell was exciting. My golf game improved. I could scorch the ball hundreds of yards off the tee. If it melted before I got to the green, I took another one from my environmentally incorrect asbestos underwear and placed it in the cup. Cheating is revered in Hell.

I didn't care much for Hell's Kitchen's food. I couldn't handle those hot peppers and sauces the devious cooks put in *everything*, including ice cream. But then I met Jeffrey Daumer. He taught me to enjoy fava beans, Chianti and his excellent human liver stew and kidney pie. He also made an excellent Devil's Food cake for dessert. I was welcome, he said, to join him on his next hunt. He had found easy prey in Saint Colony, the resort where the good and innocent people were being prepared for the journey to Heaven. I declined the offer, so he took Bonnie and Clyde instead.

Hell's TV reception was pretty good — underground cable, you know — but we only got the *Weather Channel*, two *Shopping Channels* and *Howard Stern*. The weather was always warm, of course, and we couldn't own anything anyway. But Howard gave us plenty to talk about, especially hot, kinky sex and S&M, which was bountiful down there. The piped-in music was clear as a bell in Hell, except I got tired of hearing the inspirational theme song, *Devil With the Blue Dress, Blue Dress On, Devil with the Blue Dress On*, repeated continuously. I never even saw these devils, except for the transvestites that came out of their caves once in awhile.

One day, when I was walking my dog Killer, (*a pit bull that had croaked 13 children and two postmen — but he's really very gentle*), I ran into Adolph Hitler. Yep, the real thing. And the craziest thing I ever heard, came from his mouth. "Nah, I didn't kill all those people for a purpose. It was just plain fun torturing them and watching them die. What a gig. I'm glad to see Mark Fuhrman do the right thing, too. I'm looking forward to meeting him soon."

Yes, it was quite an experience. Adolph is now working in a Hell sweat shop making pitchforks and firebombs. He told me the Hell's Army is hoping to rise up when the big earthquake hits, and take over the world. "This time," he said, "I'll get it right!"

No matter how hard I tried, I wasn't quite able to adapt to the southern culture. I wasn't really the devil my mother said I was. I hadn't done anything real bad except steal a squirt gun and lie to her a few times about taking the last chocolate-chip cookie. So when I tried joining the local chapter of Hell's Angels, it wouldn't compromise its tough standards. I was declined admittance to the club. I was too *good* for those damned fellas!

I was disappointed and angry and put in for a transfer to Heaven. I wasn't too excited about coming here at first; but when I arrived, I got my first pair of wings and took off like an angel. I crashed a few times, but after some minor adjustments, was able to mingle with the others, meandering through the fresh air like a fish in water. The sensation of peace and freedom was good, but after several months, I began hankering for something more exciting to do.

One day I stopped by at the Pearly Gates and painted them red. I thought it was fun and would get me some attention — it did. I had to turn in my wings for a week. I was grounded.

The food in Heaven isn't that great either. You just get used to it. The Angel Hair pasta is pretty good, but I couldn't find a good red sauce anywhere, (*red is a forbidden color up here*) and the Angel Food cake isn't half bad. For music, however, I preferred Hell. All the good, popular songs I was used to when I was alive, have been edited, for Heaven's sake. All the good sex and violence is gone. Angel Broadcasting System plays only soothing and melodic religious songs. Movies here suck. You can get *Heaven Can Wait, The Flying Nun, Alice in Wonderland, Bambi* and other harmless fare, but for excitement, about the only thing you can do is tell a fellow Angel to "Go to Hell" — and get grounded again.

This is severe punishment though, because without wings it's impossible to get from cloud to cloud, so you just find a nice soft spot, drift for awhile and wait it out. I've been waiting it out for several years, and only one thought keeps me from going nuts — knowing that patience is a most important virtue — something I wish I had learned while I was alive.

One glorious day I was practicing some stunt flying. I crashed. I tried to brush off the angel dust from my wings as I walked to the nearest dry cleaners. There, behind the counter, I saw my mother and father smiling. It was incredible. They had always wanted their own business.

They died when I was young and I had never expected to see them again. We talked for a long while, took a Sunday fly to *Cloud 9* and reminisced. We apologized for the many things we said and did to hurt each other and agreed nothing much should have mattered when we were alive except love, a decent dose of joy and sadness, a good meal and — just to be a little human, an occasional wrongdoing. Well, now we know.

I've asked *Big Angel*, our leader, if I could go to Hell to rehabilitate some old friends down there, but have been rejected because I hadn't accrued enough frequent flyer miles.

So I guess I'll just hang around and await your arrival. Fortunately there's plenty of space here. But take my advice. Earthly immortality, according to the Devil's Advocacy Dictionary, means giving up your spirit and soul. Don't do it! Live a full life, do something worthwhile.

Immortality in the light of Heaven beats the hell out of the dark side of the other place.

Using Remotes for Fun and Control

Some modern conveniences make my imagination run amok.
Remote controls, for example.
Everything is becoming remotely scientific.

My favorite is the VCR. I've learned, like most of you, to tape my favorite shows, then *zap* the commercials while watching the good stuff later. Eliminate huddles and beer commercials, and you can see an exciting football game in 15 minutes. When watching action movies like *Rambo*, fast forward to the action and eliminate the *yo's*, grunts and plots.

Sometimes I feel there's too much going on in the world too fast, and I'm missing out. But I have a solution.

When a child is born, implant a micro-chip in the brain. It records sights and sounds through the eyes and ears and also regulates muscles. Parents receive a remote control with a registered frequency. When the kids grow up the chip is removed. They can then get their own remote control for *their* kids. Even better, people could sell their frequencies and make lots of money.

Thinking deeply about the consequences of my insanity, the vision becomes more and more entertaining.

The other day I was talking too much about this idea to my wife. But she loved it! She suggested using the *mute* button so she wouldn't have to listen to me. I suggested using *Fast Forward* to get her to cook more often. She wasn't impressed.

I fantasize.

While playing tennis with a friend who always wins, I put him in *slow motion* and beat him easily!

I had good sex once. I play the tape over and over and over again, enjoying it alone or with some booze.

I go to a baseball game. A friend who is an electronic wizard, decodes the manager's remote control frequency for me. I over-ride him and make the players swing at the pitches *I* like, rather than what the manager likes. My team loses anyway, but I have fun playing

9

electronic games with real heroes, rather than video games with imaginary ones.

Now, if I had the frequency of everyone on earth . . .

China would be democratic. I'd *erase* the minds of the totalitarian leaders. If I caught a burglar climbing into someone's house, I'd *freeze-frame* him and call the cops to remove the body. The *mute* button would be terrific for eliminating gab from used-car and insurance salesmen, teenagers, politicians and telephone solicitors. And when I went out for fast-food, I could *fast forward* for better service. If low on funds, I could *freeze-frame* the hand reaching out for my money and speed off without paying.

If I went to a concert I could *mute* the crowd and hear the music; if traffic were too slow I could *fast-forward* the drivers and *slow-mo* the cops! And if I were interested in politics, I could manipulate politicians in Congress to abstain from voting for laws that didn't fit my fancy. Then I could become president and then . . .

I'm out of control! I'm a dictator!

Some things are better left uncontrolled. Obviously, even micro-chips can go bad.

It's something to think about if you have nothing else in your mind or are temporarily out of control.

Pillow Talk: America's Best Kept Secrets

My seductive wife whispered in my ear that I had a birthmark on the back of my neck. I frowned at learning this important news.

Then she picked a hair from inside the other ear — it didn't help me listen better, but she certainly got my attention. "Ow!"

I asked her about the mole on her little toe. She responded by rubbing the fatty waste deposits on my belly.

Intimate pillow talk like this started when we were infants. Our proud parents tickled our chins and "goo-gooed" us with our first eloquent vocabulary lesson.

Doris Day and Rock Hudson used pillows to make a movie. Spies and politicians are leery about who they sleep with for fear of revealing secrets of their personal behavior which they might read about in the tabloids.

"Honey, I need some 'waa-waa.' I'm thirsty."

My wife's reply? "Do waa, do waa, do waa diddy. Get up and get it yourself." We enjoyed the quick, child-like exchange.

We looked at each other and wondered what other couples talk about in bed. We figured most people talk about similar things and, from time to time, if they get lucky and feel good, are moaning "Oooh, aaah," instead of saying "goo-goo."

Unless, of course, they are the president and first lady. People held in such high esteem are above such trivial conversation.

———————————

"George," said Martha to the famous general, "I really don't like running my hand through your wig. It's terribly tangled, and that awful powder gets in my eyes. Can't you take it off in bed? And please, George, don't nibble my ears with those awful wooden teeth!"

"Fine, Martha. Then you stop complaining about my dirty clothes. I can't help it if the Potomac was muddy when I crossed during that storm."

"Abe, I'm so proud you freed the slaves," said Mary. "But how much longer will I have to mend your clothes, wash the dishes, cook, answer all your letters and pay the bills?"

"You're absolutely right dear. I'll see about freeing women in my next term or in a 100 years, whichever comes first."

"Jimmy, do you still lust for other women?" asked Rosalyn.

"Well, gee, yes, dear. But *only* when I'm not with you."

"Well if you really love me, please make Billy pick up his empty beer cans. I almost killed myself the other night when I stumbled on one after he left. And stop leaving peanut shells in bed. Just look at these scratches on my thighs."

"Oh, Rosalyn — ummmm."

11

"Pat, I'm in the mood for love. How about you?" asked Richard of his wife.

"I'm always here for you dear, but do you have to tape everything we say? It could be so embarrassing."

"Not to worry, honey. I'm really good at operating these tape machines. I can save the good stuff just for us."

"Jackie, I can't find a thing to wear tomorrow for my birthday. The closet's so full of your designer clothes, we need another closet."

"Wear your birthday suit, Jack. I heard rumors Marilyn is going to sing for you."

"Huh? Who? What? Uh, oh!"

"Lyndon, would you *please* put that cigarette out. It's stinking up the place!"

"Yeah, yeah, yeah, Lady Bird. Sometimes I just want to (*expletive, expletive*) and then (*expletive, expletive*) and I'm tired of hearing your (*expletive, expletive*). Hey, wanna see my scar again?"

"Gerald, I could really go for another hug when you're done reading the paper in there."

"Right, Betty. I'm almost finished. I still have to soak my sore ankle from that stumble in the elevator. Why don't you have a few more drinks while you're waiting?"

"Ronnie, are you awake? Honey, I'd like a good-night kiss. Honey, wake up!"

"Sorry Nancy. I was just resting my eyes. Is it time to make love already? Geez, I forgot. It's been a month?"

"Ronnie, my astrologer said that tonight the moon and stars are placed just right for a successful, romantic evening."

"Good, honey. Call Sinatra and see what he's got planned. I could go for some late-night entertainment, too."

"George, my back is killing me. I think we need a new mattress. There are bulges everywhere."

"Don't worry, Barbara. It's just our life savings. Jeb said it's safer here than in his bank."

"Hillary, I'm really enjoying this job. But I can't sneak a Big Mac through the Secret Service net or order a pizza. The phone doesn't work."

"Don't worry, Bill. I've got a team of unemployed Jack-In-The-Box people working in a secret kitchen buried under the Rose Garden. They can fix pizzas and fried chicken, too."

———————————

Pillow talk is still one of America's best kept secrets. Nobody really cares what regular folks talk about.

Be thankful!

The Ultimate Real People *Fitness Program*

I looked in the mirror after hobbling out of the shower. It's not appropriate to describe what I saw, but it was cause for an emergency visit to my physical fitness counselor.

I met Rebecca at the gym. Her office is on the second floor, so when I got there I smiled with difficulty, trying to obscure heavy breathing. The breath mints were ineffective, too.

"Well," she said, "I'm glad you've finally decided your life is worth living. I'm sure you'll quit smoking when you start on your program again."

Rebecca was very pleasant, as usual, explaining how the muscle groups in the body worked. I still don't remember much of what she said because I was observing some of the better muscular specimens working out in the training area downstairs.

"When you're able to complete 15 repetitions of each without pain, you'll begin seeing a difference," she explained. "But you must also walk fast at least three miles, three times a week to condition your heart and lungs."

I asked feebly. "Can I smoke if I walk slowly?" She scowled.

Rebecca reminded me to eat vegetables, low-fat foods and drink plenty of water. I remembered why I visited only occasionally.

I thanked her for the good advice and left, leaving behind those sweat-soaked heroes on the machines I knew I wouldn't see for another year. I was exhausted from the experience.

When I got home, I put together a *real people* health and fitness program I could maintain. Of course, I was under the influence of Haagen Dazs when I wrote it.

MONDAY: Drink six-pack of beer. Fill empty cans with sand. Lift each 100 times. Strengthen biceps to prepare for Miller Lite commercial audition.

TUESDAY: Dine at McDonald's. Carefully drop 16 French fries on the floor. Pick each one up separately, walk to the garbage and trash it. Strengthen lower back, reduce fat intake, demonstrate politically-correct environmental technique.

WEDNESDAY: Turn on early-morning, TV aerobic-exercise program. Sit in recliner. Put tray of chocolate-chip cookies at least six feet away. Eat one at each commercial. Good for legs, back, heart, lungs and discipline.

THURSDAY: Go to health-food store. Park across street next to Colonel Sanders. Carry each bag of groceries back to car, one at a time. Good for heart, lungs, biceps and triceps. Eat bucket of chicken before returning home to eat vegetables in front of family. Good for you!

FRIDAY: Celebrate surviving another week. Invite neighbors and their kids over for dessert. Take kids in backyard to play hide and seek. Make kids hide while you seek the dessert. Good fun and excellent way to train kids.

SATURDAY: Take three-mile walk to park. Carry fully-equipped picnic basket: potato chips, beer, fried chicken and cookies. Shift basket from one arm to the other, lifting it up and down while walking. Excellent aerobics. Good for biceps. Eat fast to exercise jaw muscles and strengthen stomach. Jog back to car with picnic basket massaging protruding stomach. Burn off excess calories.

SUNDAY: Review week's progress. Read newspaper recipe section. Read exercise and diet books and listen to inspirational *Rocky* music. Then do nothing! Begin the regimen again on Monday.

There you have it, the ultimate, realistic, guilt-free physical fitness guide — no designer work-out clothes, health club dues or body punishment.

McDonald's, Burger King and Colonel Sanders have always been my favorite exercise spas — in and out of the car, to the counter, to the table, back to the car.

I hope this program works for you. In the meantime, I'm looking for one of those carnival mirrors that will make me look good after my next shower!

Let the Slow Lane Olympics Begin!

I love the Olympics.

The thrill of victory, the agony of defeat.

Who thinks launching your body over a pole with a bent bamboo stick is better than watching someone *else* do it on TV? *I do!*

Why? Because I *can't* do it. So I figure there's a need for a new competition — one for those of us who don't meet the physical or mental qualifications of real athletes.

No need to negotiate a TV contract or advertising rates. Let the Slow Lane Games begin!

EVENTS

YAWNING — Dogs line up in a straight row, judged on their ability to demonstrate the arrogant ignoring of the enticing antics of their masters to make them do ridiculous tricks. Technical points deducted for any movement other than yawns.

DIAPER CHANGING — Husband and wife teams are judged on ability to remove and replace disposable diapers while their children are feeding. Points deducted for crying (*the baby's, not the parents'*); extra points awarded if the victim smiles.

COUPON CLIPPING — Stacks of newspaper coupons are piled up in front of combatants. Scissors and Xacto knives are provided. The fastest at clipping 35 grocery items, in order of price and total value, wins. Points deducted for duplicates, torn coupons and dismembered fingers.

DISH WASHING — Twelve settings of fine china and silver are covered with melted cheese, eggs, peanut butter and spaghetti. Contestants are provided with rubber gloves, SOS pads and scouring powder. Deductions for soap streaks, scratches and water spots.

PAINT DRYING — A wall is painted with six colors of water-based paint. Contestants are judged on self control while watching the paint dry. Points deducted for any body movement or break in eye contact with the empty wall.

LEAF RAKING — Contestants are buried under two tons of leaves and provided with rakes and snorkels. First contestant to fill 42 trash bags, wins. Points taken off for broken leaves or use of hands.

CAR WASHING — Six 1939 Fords are doused with mud and oil. Contestants prepare cars for the International Classic Auto Show. Winner decided by cleanest car in 30-minute time limit. Points deducted for use of soap or wax.

TV WATCHING — Contestants are required to watch giant TVs for 24 uninterrupted hours. Winners must watch all commercials, public television documentaries, political speeches, editorial commentaries and the *Weather Channel*. Points deducted for any interest in the programming or taking eyes off the screen.

GROCERY SHOPPING MARATHON — Each contestant is given $500 to spend, $100 at each of five grocery stores within a 50-mile radius. The contestant must return to the starting point within six hours. Winner will be chosen based on the total numbers of cucumbers, oranges, packages of toilet paper, tubes of toothpaste and pounds of extra-lean ground beef bought. Winners of coupon-clipping contest are not eligible.

When the Slow Lane Olympics become popular throughout the world, winners will be flown to Hollywood to film commercial endorsements for products involved with their winning event.

It's about time normal people are recognized world-wide for *their* extraordinary abilities too!

Pardon Me, Mr. President, Did You Find My Golf Ball?

Executives use company expense accounts to play golf because it's the best way to seal a deal. The fresh air and relaxed environment, they claim, stimulates honest and constructive dialogue.

Presidents Bush, Clinton and Ford linked up to play golf recently at the *Bob Hope Desert Classic* in Palm Springs. The trio allegedly resolved important political issues with its collective wisdom and personal rapport, while searching for stray golf balls.

But a little birdie told me otherwise. The day really went something like this.

———————

"You're first Gerry. Give it a rip," says Willie. Whack! The ball sails into the trees. "Boy, did I clobber that one. Anyone see where it went?"

George and Willie shrug their shoulders. "What club did you drive with?" asks Willie.

"The *Big Betty*. Got it at the *Clinic's* souvenir store. Autographed, too!"

Whack! Willie hits it even further into the trees.

"Geez, what club is that?" asks George.

"It's the *Big Smoker*. A college buddy gave it to me."

Smack! George hits the ball down the middle. "*Big Lips*. It reads fairways real well," smiles George.

17

"Hey, what's the bet?" asks Willie.

"Well, if you win," says George, "I'll campaign for you in'96. If I win, you'll join me on the *Montel Williams' Show* and admit I was the better president."

"What about if I win?" asks Gerry.

"We'll both give up golf," chuckle Willie and George.

On the fourth hole, Willie picks up his red cellular phone to order lunch from McDonald's.

"Nice shot, George. Ooops! Thought it was on the green. Looks like you hit the sand," says Willie. They approach the green.

"I like sand shots. I'm good at them," says George. He steps confidently into the trap, smiles, looks down at the ball. Whack! He hits it onto the green. It rolls into the cup.

"Great shot!" says Gerry. "There should be a law against lucky shots like that," says the frustrated Willie.

George smiles. "Nobody beats me in the sand, nobody," he says triumphantly, showing his partners his personalized ball with the dour face of Saddam Hussein on it.

At the sixth hole, Willie hits a long iron shot into the water hazard. "Sorry about that, Bill," says George. "You should stay clear of white water."

"Very funny George." The Big Macs arrive. George and Willie gorge quickly, chortling as they wait for Gerry who's stumbling on the steps of the spectator stand trying to get his ball loose from an overhanging tree branch.

On the eighth hole, George bends over suddenly on the green. "Oh geez. My stomach doesn't feel right. Oh my!" He loses his lunch behind a clump of trees.

"That's not environmentally correct, George," says Willie.

"Pardon me, pardon me please," begs George.

"Okay, Okay. I can be good at that," says Gerry proudly as he trots over to George.

"What happened?" George moans.

"Oh, sorry George. Forgot to tell you. Hillary wants me to be healthier, so now I order Big Macs without cheese."

"So?" asks George.

"Well, umm, I use sliced broccoli instead." Willie turns away, hiding a big smirk.

George and Willie stand on the tee of the 18th hole. Gerry, out of the competition, is still looking for his ball that bounced off a spectator's forehead on the 17th.

"Well George, should we wait for him or go ahead?"

"No, let's go. I've got my big boat docked at that lake by the green over there. Got a couple poles and shotguns too. We can do a little hunting and fishing while we wait."

"Great idea, George. I haven't sunk a birdie or eagle all day!"

The trio is joined by Bob Hope in the clubhouse.

"Who won?" asks Bob.

Willie prevaricates. "We tied. The environment was so conducive to important dialogue on policy issues, we resolved our differences but forgot to keep our golf scores."

"Fantastic! This means you'll play at my tournament again next year?"

"Maybe," says George. "We also agreed taxpayers would resent us for using our government expense accounts for golf unless we made significant progress toward world peace."

"Absolutely," says Bob. "That's why I've invited nine world leaders next year. Hussein, Arafat, Yeltzin and Streisand have already accepted the challenge. It should be an entertaining atmosphere for resolving world problems."

"Streisand? I'll be there," says Willie. "What will you call the big event?"

"The *Bob Hope Tournament of Practical Jokes.*"

Truth in Dying: It's a Dead Issue

I was shocked and irritated by the unsolicited sales call.

The phone rang during *Wheel of Fortune* just as I was about to impress my wife with the winning phrase, "Saved by the Bell."

Normally I don't mind sales calls too much because I'm good at saying, "No, I'm not interested," after listening only to the first six words. I learned this important skill playing *Name That Tune*.

This particular call, however, kept my interest. The first six words; "Sir, we're offering free burial . . ." got my attention. I'm serious. I listened carefully as the woman continued. "If you buy a plot for a loved one now, you'll receive another one for yourself absolutely free."

At first I laughed. She didn't respond. So I went along with her deadly pitch.

"I'm not dying to get into a cemetery at this time," I said. "Where do you get the nerve to call people like this?"

"Well sir, at Sleepy Lake's Slumberland Cemetery, we seriously believe that life after death can be both peaceful and exciting. If you're interested, sir, we'll send you our color brochure showing our beautiful grounds near the lake or the airport, or how about the golf course and the shopping mall? Wouldn't you like to be buried in close proximity to these exciting places so you and your loved ones will always be in good spirits? None of our clients has ever complained. That's why it's easy to make this once-in-a-lifetime offer." She obviously had practiced her lines a lot.

"Funny. Does the undertaker have a sense of humor?"

"Oh no, sir. He takes his job very seriously except when he has friends for dinner."

"Oh God! You're sick, lady! I don't want to hear anymore about your special offer. Good bye."

"Before you go, keep in mind you get your choice of location and schedule whenever you want your Sleepy Lake's Slumber Box moved. This option is offered at no extra cost if you commit before your next birthday or passing, whichever comes first."

"Hmmm. I can be buried on top of my wife?"

"Certainly. Unless of course, she prefers the top and selects her plot before you do."

"And I can be moved any time next to *anyone* I choose?"

"Yes. We provide a catalog showing photos and biographies of others that have already signed up."

"I see. Hmmm. After being married for so many years I guess enjoying a couple of fantasies with a few acquaintances from around town wouldn't be too unreasonable."

"We don't condone such behavior, sir, but it's certainly a *very* common practice."

"Okay. How much does your service cost?"

"Sir, we can't give prices over the telephone. You'll have to come in first and select your Slumber Box and plot preferences. Lakefront property, as you probably know, is more expensive."

Aren't coffins all pretty much the same?"

"Not anymore, sir. We now have them with antennas and modem-equipped, lap-top computers. Many clients believe communication with relatives is more convenient with on-line seances. We offer others with inboard motors for lakeside fishing or spiritual recreation. Some are outfitted with ATMs for those who like to take it with them, if you know what I mean, and others are equipped with Las Vegas-style slot machines."

"Ha! And I suppose there are some made for space flight?"

"No, but we do have a few with out-of-this-world, virtual-reality games."

The offer was beginning to sound too good to be true.

"This has been lots of fun lady. But I gotta get back to the TV or I'll miss my favorite Charles Bronson movie."

"Which one?"

"*Death Wish.* Ha, ha. Pretty funny, huh? You thought you had me believing your ridiculous sales pitch. Thought I was pretty stupid, didn't you? Well I got news for you. I knew this was a scam."

"What makes you say that?"

"Everything you said made sense and sounded fun. But when you referred to a Slumber Box with an inboard motor, I knew something was deadly wrong."

"Why?"

"The exhaust fumes would *kill* anyone inside a closed box!"

I still can't understand why she hung up.

Matching Facts and Fiction When Convenient

I couldn't sleep. I was dreaming — nothing unusual for someone known to stretch facts farther than a politician or Texas fisherman. You know about dreams — If you don't write them down immediately you forget all the details.

So, it's 4:45 a.m., it's snowing, I'm at the computer in my tiny room. A space heater is fanning out hot air, forcing the smoke from my pipe to swirl artfully among the cobwebs. I'm sipping a hot, stimulating, triple espresso. This time, I'm writing it down. It's too important to forget.

I was just ordained King of the World by intelligent world leaders who recognize my wisdom and leadership abilities. I've been provided with unlimited wealth in exchange for my services.

Wait a minute. Wait. Facts and fiction. As I re-read the first paragraphs here, I was hit by the truth, which generally, is boring — that's why I exaggerate. It was actually 5:15 a.m. when I started writing, and the smoke smells like a cow barn. The snow? It's only a frost. The dream? Not accurate either.

The truth is, I was lying awake thinking what it would be like to be the Sultan of Brunei, the richest man in the world, who recently flew into Seattle in his private 747 for the APEC meeting. He *is* the supreme leader of his country and worth a reported $37 billion. Now *that's* an *enormous* fact!

But for those of us living ordinary lives, facts must be exaggerated or we wouldn't be very interesting. What ordinary citizen would be a good TV talk show guest or a charismatic politician? That's why most of us have a gym bag of rubber facts stretched by very loose memories.

I confess.

I didn't really hit a grand-slam homer in the bottom of the 6th inning of the Little League World Series as I've told people all my life. I *did* strike out, though, in a hometown minor-league game, and the winning run scored when the catcher dropped the ball.

My wife didn't really beg me to marry her. She felt sorry for me — I couldn't get anybody else. But she also believed my Swiss bank account story. I didn't win the *Most Popular* award in high school either. But I accepted the embarrassment like a man when presented with the symbolic toilet brush for *Least Likely to Succeed.*

And no, I didn't really give up lucrative careers as a brain surgeon or crooked politician to become a columnist.

Flexible facts and good story ideas, which may or may not be true, still make interesting conversation if you can find somebody willing to listen.

Clint Eastwood has never shot a real gun in his life, and the Pope lusted for Margaret Thatcher. Secretary of State Warren Christopher can't smile because his foot is stuck in his mouth. The IRS audited itself and now its agents must pay off the national debt.

My neighbor, a recently-retired volunteer fire chief, heralded as a community leader, was really convicted as a child for opening fire hydrants during a heat wave. He was ordered by a strict judge to serve in the appropriate community service for life.

Rush Limbaugh and Dan Quayle both dated Candace Bergen, but were rejected for being too liberal, and Whoopi Goldberg, judged by members of the Klu Klux Klan, won the *Most Beautiful Conservative* award over Whitney Houston and Diana Ross.

Rhode Island is claiming historical territorial dominion over New York, Pennsylvania, New Hampshire, Vermont, Maine, and Ohio to gain bragging rights as the country's largest state. Texas and

ADVENTURES IN THE SLOW LANE

Alaska left the U.S., proving crude oil and cow chips are enough to sustain an entire country.

Michael Jordan, O.J. Simpson and Mohammed Ali are *not* the most recognizable names in the world. John Doe, in English-speaking countries, and Mr. Lee in Asian countries, are far more common. It's true that Thursday once followed Sunday, until somebody proved God couldn't create such a mess in only four days.

Imagination is more powerful, entertaining, controversial and exciting than the truth, which is only what we believe it is anyway. So why bother with it?

That's what makes politicians and fiction writers so interesting, entertaining and frequently ridiculous.

I'm going back to sleep to dream up more profound ideas.

Getting "Cultured" at the Ballet

I feel better knowing I've finally attained "cultured" status — I went to the ballet recently.

Years ago, when I was in Texas drinking with the "good ole boys," I was ashamed to admit my curiosity about *dancing swans* and *nutcracker suites*, so I kept my mouth shut or filled it with beer and whiskey. When I lived in Europe I was embarrassed to say I had *never even been to the ballet*, so I kept my mouth shut or filled it with pasta and bread.

And it's been no easy ride anywhere else because most of my three friends have always questioned my bohemian sense of fashion and barbaric manner of speaking. But now that I've attained this new, upper-class status, it would be a blatant act of selfishness not to pass along my new knowledge. (*Actually, I promised to promote the ballet for our new performing arts center in exchange for free tickets, the use of the director's coat and tie and a free meal*).

24

One of the interesting aspects of ballet is you never know who or what the star is. You can't remember the names. This is good, because you must concentrate solely on the performances. But Galina Mezentseva, the star ballerina they called *Prima* for short, stood out among other performers Elena Poryvkina, Elena Chokhine, Elizaveta Ananian and Tatiana Chanina. There is no room for sexism in ballet; except for the over-sized Haines jock straps, you'd never know Alexander Makarov and Anatoly Semenove were male performers.

I was amazed by the grace, flexibility and acrobatic movements of all the dancers. The music was pretty good too. I had heard of Tchaikovsky, Rachmaninoff and Paganini, but didn't associate them with dancing. When the recorded, *Music Classic Disco* was played, I felt more comfortable.

During intermission, I asked the woman next to me if she knew about ballet. She replied with a heavy accent, "I think so. I'm a prima ballerina in the Bolshoi." I had heard of that Russian dance group, so I quickly got her autograph. She had to be authentic because her signature looked something like an *Elena.* "Have you ever danced with anybody I'd know?" I asked. She mentioned a couple guys named Nerviev and Brushnicough, something like that. "I know them!" I said gleefully. "Aren't they the guys who taught John Travolta to dance in *Saturday Night Fever!*" I asked her to explain what some of the most difficult dance steps were. She declined with an evil glare.

I was excited about the ballet experience. I really wanted to learn about the dance movements, so I did some research. A simple *Assemble* is when you go up and down, kicking one leg out to the front, side or back while the other leg does the jumping. If you can put yourself back together, you've successfully completed the movement. A *Ballon* means "bounce." It's the quality of a smooth ascent and descent in jumping, achieved primarily by the pliant use of the feet. If you don't explode when landing, you are able to continue into the next movement called a *Batterie.*

This is a term referring to beating the feet together or crossing them in the air to add brilliance to jumping steps. If this is done correctly, the dancer gets energized to do an *Elevation,* whereby he or she jumps high into the air, acting suspended. If this isn't done properly, the performer falls flat on his or her face and is escorted backstage in disgrace. But this rarely happens. In jumps more than three feet high, the *Tutu,* that interesting skirt that sticks straight out, is used as a parachute. Men are less fortunate.

I was glad to learn the famous *Nutcracker Suite* was named after a dancer many years ago. The leotard he borrowed from one of the ladies was way too tight. After performing the difficult, scissors-like leg maneuver called a *Sissonne,* he fell to the ground, writhing in pain. I also found out that 16 young, female dancers had once brawled on stage to obtain the prima ballerina title for an upcoming, untitled performance. The choreographer was so impressed with the graceful movements of flailing arms and legs and the puddle of sweat on the hardwood floor, he appropriately named the ballet, *Swan Lake.*

I'm excited about becoming even more cultured. I hope to continue my education. With the free publicity and insight into ballet I've provided here, I'm hoping the executive director of the performing arts center will provide me with another freebie for the next opera that's coming to town.

If not, I'll continue investigating *Rapping.*

Housefly More Dangerous Than Cruise Missiles

Cruise missiles only irritate Saddam Hussein, perhaps inviting his retaliation on a grander scale. But a common housefly made a more immediate and personal impression upon me, and *did get* retaliation!

Here I was, slumping comfortably on my squeaky swivel chair preparing to write a column of great importance on the ramifications of the U S attack on Iraq. I stared intently at the screen waiting for great words to appear. Then, without warning, this bold, arrogant housefly lit upon the glass.

I missed! The back of my hand scratched the screen (*I had told my wife I didn't need a wedding ring*), and I could actually see footprints in the dust where the fly had given *Top Gun* new meaning with its smooth and belligerent take-off.

The chase began.

I ran to the kitchen, grabbing the Texas-sized fly-swatter. I opened my secret desk compartment where I store the household arsenal of rubber-band, squirt and fly guns. The latter quickly shoots a circular, plastic *masher* in the direction of its target.

I heard the buzz in the kitchen, but couldn't see the critter. My visual radar couldn't track the Stealth Raider and my human ears quickly lost contact.

Silence.

He was on the venetian blinds by the kitchen table. Wham! The gun blasted. I missed, knocking over the vase, spilling the water and flowers onto the floor.

I reloaded and waited. Nothing. I went back into my office. I took a break and started writing. "The cruise missile attack was . . ."

"Bzzzz . . . Bzzzz . . . Zzzt."

The menace returned. I closed the office door, trapping him. He couldn't get out now! I sat down. He circled overhead. I waited, hoping he'd find a safe landing zone on the window where I'd have a clear shot.

Again, silence.

I remained motionless. "Bzzz . . . Bzzz . . . ." He provoked me to get up from the chair. Whap! I swung the folded newspaper at the top of the desk where he had made an unscheduled stop. Damn! Ow! Missed again! I thought I broke my toe, stubbing it on the chair leg. I wasn't happy, either, that I'd knocked the small overhead desk lamp down, breaking the bulb and getting slivers of glass in my bare foot. But a warrior feels no pain!

ADVENTURES IN THE SLOW LANE

The silence was annoying. I started writing again. "Saddam Hussein must be laughing now at the ineffective results of the latest bombing raid, but he's . . ."

I welcomed the evening darkness. I turned on the light and waited. "Bzzz . . . Bzzz . . . Zzzzt."

Gotcha! I watched him frolic around the ceiling light as I left the office, closing the door behind. Surely, he'd kill himself with exhaustion during the night, and all I'd have to do is pick up his carcass in the morning.

I'd finish writing, in peace, the next day.

"Good night, dear."

"Good night," said my wife.

My dreams weren't pleasant. I heard buzzes that weren't. I woke up and went into the kitchen to sneak the last piece of chocolate cake.

Zzzzaap! A buzz that was! He landed directly on the frosting in the "no-fly zone." I threw the cake against the wall. "Take *that*, you ugly fly!"

Finally, he's dead!

I went back to bed.

"What was that?"

"Nothing, dear, nothing."

I closed my eyes.

"Bzzzz . . . Bzzzz . . . Zzzzt."

"Damn! Damn! Damn!"

I jumped out of bed, grabbed the fly-swatter, fly gun, newspaper and baseball bat! Enough was enough. It was 3 a.m. — not the best time to irritate an irritable writer.

I ran into the bathroom, splashed cold water on my face, put on my slippers — and then — oh, no! I slipped in the puddle of vase water by the kitchen table I had never mopped up.

My back hurt and my wrist twinged with pain. (*"Expletive, expletive, expletive"*).

I turned off all the lights except the night stand lamp.

28

"Don't worry, honey, I've got everything under control. Get under the covers and don't move. Everything will be all right."

I stepped quietly into the closet, leaving a crack in the door. I watched. I listened. I waited. Yes, yes, yes. He took the bait!

He wasn't moving. There he was, big, bold and ugly. Then he took a quick "fly-by" *(A term used by ace pilots and punsters)* around the shapely target hidden under the blankets.

Then he landed on the lamp shade. I was ready. I was determined. I was *angry!*

I pushed the door open, ran out and *smash!* He had no chance. The war was over. Peace at last!

"Yikes, honey! What was that?"

"I got 'em, I got 'em. Yeah, yeah!" I put the bat down.

My wife was crying. "And how are we going to replace my grandmother's lamp?"

I left the bedroom, energized by the success of my mission, to finish the column. Morning light cast a calm shadow across the window shades. "And someday, Mr. Hussein will retaliate for the petty annoyances with a vengeance never recorded before . . ."

Oh God! I paused. There on the window, resting comfortably, was the big, ugly, persistent and devastating fly.

I wrote quickly.

"In the end Saddam Hussein will terminate his own rule. He will leave Iraq hastily to preserve what little sanity he has before being tormented to death by the nuisances of U.N inspection teams and cruise missiles."

I slammed the door and ran into the garage.

I called my wife from Alaska. "I need some time alone."

She understood.

29

Before Crossing a Border, Cross Your Fingers

I was the kid who always got caught sneaking across the borders of Mrs. Marple's rose garden — a shortcut to the soda shop. The thorns were attracted to my cotton shirts, so I stopped frequently to free myself while so-called friends laughed and got away.

Mrs. Marple was kinder than the U.S. border guards I met returning from a recent ski trip to Canada. Her warm smile and raised eyebrows warned me to be careful and much more sneaky the next time I violated her boundaries without permission.

Not so with the cold, suspicious, uniformed professionals guarding the borders.

On the way into Canada I had bought an illegal quantity of alcoholic beverages at the duty-free store. I laughed when my friend Scott warned me to follow the rules. "How will they know?"

A week later we were returning home. I intended to buy some more tax-free alcoholic beverages at the Canadian duty-free store — you know, gifts for friends and special occasions like when you can't find cold water or beer. My wife and Scott warned me again, but arrogantly I said, "What's another couple of bottles? What can they do, arrest me? Make me pay the taxes?"

At the store, I pulled into the exit instead of the entrance. It was dark. Somewhat embarrassed, I backed up and made it safely into the parking lot. "Why don't you take off your sun glasses?" asked my wife.

"Because my regular glasses are in a bag somewhere in the trunk. I'll get them later. Besides, I can see fine."

So I bought four bottles, then drove several yards to the booth at the border crossing. The man with the Official Sneer poked out his head. "Where ya headed?"

"Home," I said.

"Where were you?"

"Skiing at Whistler Mountain." He peered into the car, looking us over carefully.

"How long?"

"Just a couple of hours, sir. I'm a pretty lousy skier." I chuckled feebly at my own joke. For some reason, no one joined me.

"Do you have anything to declare?"

"Yes officer. I have a bottle of wine, a six-pack of Coca-Cola and another joke. Would you like to hear it?" I was trying to cover up my fear of impending doom. It didn't work.

"Pull over and park there."

I was going to jail! My clean slate was tarnished forever.

I parked next to the important-looking building with all the government symbols and stuff painted and etched onto the stucco. "Oh geez, honey. Keep the payments on my golf clubs current. Tell your mom I couldn't make her birthday party because I broke my leg. Tell Lars and Marlene I can't make dinner because I caught the flu! Tell the editors I broke my hands tumbling down the steepest hill."

In the gloomy lobby, another officer with a drab, wrinkled uniform and matching face, took all of our driver's licenses, cautiously comparing our faces to the photos. He pointed to a tarnished wooden bench. "Wait there." I melted into a panic.

My forehead and hands were sweating. My body quivered. My wife told me to put the baseball cap on properly instead of backwards and take off my dark glasses. I had never broken the law before except when *accidentally* cheating a little on taxes and trespassing on Mrs. Marple's property.

Waiting was difficult. Scott just shook his head. "He probably watched you driving up to the store." My wife added, "I've always said you look like a criminal the way you dress."

I whispered to Scott. "Here's the keys. Grab those four bottles and trash 'em. Hurry." Too late.

"Sir." The officer beckoned me to the counter. It was all over! I closed my eyes and thought warmly of Mrs. Marple. But even my crossed fingers weren't going to get me across *this* border.

Surprise! "You can go now. I'm sorry for the delay, but we stop cars randomly to apprehend criminals."

I felt better knowing our border with Canada is secure. If you're a major criminal or just a minor, lucky one who wears dark glasses at night and drives the wrong way into one-way entrances to buy too much booze, watch out! They'll catch you.

Now that I was free again, I hoped all my friends would really enjoy their illegal booty.

It's easier trying your luck to escape taxes in April than trying it at border crossings — even if you cross your fingers.

Digging Holes, Digging Life — Dirty Games, Indeed

I received a promotional package last week from a company marketing a filthy educational video, *i dig dirt.*

It's aimed at children 2-12, so I was able to understand most of the really important stuff about how giant tractors dig holes in the ground. I even answered three of six quiz questions correctly at the end of the 30-minute program.

I don't wonder anymore why Mother didn't give us bigger tools for the sand box. One of the earth-movers cost $50 million. It was shown to be larger than six whales or eight elephants, and probably the entire stomach of George Foreman. (*Still not enough to move the dirt in Washington D.C.).* Another heap of steel had 8,000 pound tires, a 400-gallon capacity radiator and a 2,200 horsepower engine — enough to drive any youngster away from dreams of becoming a firefighter, dancer or over-paid athlete. Tractor driving is definitely the thing to do.

I got hooked on the theme song the *Children of the Dirt* were singing to the tune of *Frere Jacques.* I could follow along because of the little bouncing ball over the words.

"*I dig dirt, yes I do, yes I do. Scoop it in a shovel, drop it in a pile, pick up more, pick up more.* " I can't get this dirty song out of my head. I immediately ordered six copies for my dirty father-in-law who bales hay and is the proud owner of two real tractors. He'll enjoy watching the tape and be happy to pass along his knowledge and enthusiasm about dirt to his grandchildren at Christmas time.

I endorse this idea of producing educational videos for 2-12 year-olds. I can understand life's possibilities better from this type of video than I could from most of my college classes. Therefore, as a community service, I'm offering this video idea for anyone interested in acquiring knowledge the old fashioned way — by learning it.

I DIG LIFE — This cartoon illustrates how a happy little sperm swims upstream to meet his mate and begin a lasting and meaningful relationship. They grow together, sharing everything in common in a paradise of irresponsible bliss. Quiz question 1. *Why does the sperm do all the physical work and the egg just sits there and waits?*

I DIG FOOD — In part two of the series, we see how proper nourishment builds strong, healthy bodies. On a large treadmill, little broccoli, carrot and mushroom warriors fight a deadly battle with barbarian hamburger, ice cream, potato chip and cookie monsters. Quiz question 2. *What does a mushroom warrior have in common with a barbarian potato chip?*

I DIG LOVE — Two teenage potato-aliens with little feet, baggy clothes and big mouths, are shown shopping for space suits in a K-Mart store. Unable to find their size on the bargain racks, the male points upward with a long, red, glowing finger and says, "phone home, phone home?" The female smiles, pulls out her personal pocket computer-video and modems for new clothes through the *Alien Shopping Channel.* Delighted by her shopping skills, the male shows her his Universal Credit Card. She grins. They take off together in his spaceship on a galactic shopping spree. Quiz question 3. *Why are love and shopping similar?*

I DIG DIVORCE — Caricatures of familiar and believable couples like The Donald and Ivana, and Elizabeth Taylor and Mickey Rooney with their many ex's, cleverly illustrate why the victims are all still alive and doing quite well anyway, thank you. Quiz question 4. *What is the secret to a long life?*

I DIG LOVE II — After the divorce video we return to the basics. We learn early dating behavior and rules of courtship from Kermit the Frog and Miss Piggy. They clearly illustrate love is blind. Quiz Question 5. *Why do people get married in the first place?*

I DIG MONEY — Uncle Scrooge narrates from inside his vault. As he wallows in his loot, he explains how happiness and money go hand in hand. Quiz question 6. *Which hand should you keep your money in?*

If you dig quizzes and prizes, answer the six questions and give the correct answers to someone who cares. If you're just curious, here are the answers. 1) *The male shows aggression at a very early age.* 2) *They both look ridiculous battling without legs on a treadmill.* 3) *They both require good taste and the money to pay for it.* 4) *Prenuptial agreements and short marriages.* 5) *So they can get divorced.* 6) *The one in someone else's deep pocket.*

The prize? An educational video aimed at kids aged 30-100, titled: *I DIG READING CYNICAL WRITERS.*

At Home Where the Buffalo Roam

I recently buffaloed the doctor with a tall tale.

He had earlier ordered me to eat good food, quit my sleep demonstration job at the mattress store and to stop smoking. All heart doctors say the same thing; "Change your life-style." To them, I say, "Change your mind."

"How are you doing?" he asked.

"Well," I said, "I gave up sleep for an active desk job; I don't eat pizza, ice cream or beef, unless I'm hungry after the fruits and vegetables; and I don't inhale the pipe smoke unless I'm caught in the car during snowstorms."

Then I briefed him on my latest discovery.

"Actually, doc, I'm eating about six pounds of buffalo meat every week. It tastes better than beef. I make patties for breakfast, buff-burgers for lunch and have a small steak or roast for dinner."

His eyes narrowed. He stared at me. "Uh, huh."

I educated him.

"Well, doc, let me tell you a story. My wife was getting upset with my irritable demeanor — you know, giving up the things I like just for my health. So, to calm me down, she sent me to the grocery store to buy more healthy things to eat. I watched 600 frenzied people grabbing for packages at the meat counter. It was buffalo meat on sale during a special promotion. Six bucks a pound. I asked this elderly lady if it was good. She said it was, but I could get it cheaper at Mort's Meat Market or rustle a whole animal from the state fair like she did — or better still, go to a buffalo farm.

"So, at first, I got 10 pounds of frozen patties from Mort. He told me each four-ounce patty had only 124 calories and about 10 percent fat. That's pretty healthy, wouldn't you say? Well even my wife liked it, but I started eating the expensive stuff so regularly I depleted her shopping budget. Then *she* became irritable. Finally, we visited Ruth and Paul who own Emerald Acres, the local buffalo farm. We went there to buy direct, got a good deal and learned about the majestic animal.

"They proudly showed us a giant buffalo skin bedspread, a buffalo horn that makes music, a buffalo-hair sweater and a pair of leather shoes. Then they handed my wife this cute, little leather hat — looked good, real soft, she said. As I was about to take it, they said it was made from . . . well, needless to say, doc, I didn't touch it. Those buffalo bulls must be awfully strong. My wife got to buy all her Christmas gifts, so she returned to her normal calm self.

"We went outside for our first look at a live animal. Murphy came running down the hill to the electrified fence to eat oats from the bucket Ruth was holding. Wow, was he big! Beautiful too. But when I tried to pet him, he snorted and I got injured. Well, the electric shock wasn't too bad, but the embarrassment hurt a lot. When that buffalo smiled, I knew I'd have to get even.

"We all got into a pick-up. As we drove to the home where the buffalo roam, Paul explained they can run faster than horses, pivot on all four legs and jump over six-foot fences with ease. So when Murphy jumped the fence and followed us into the pasture, I proved my heart and courage were still intact. I jumped off the truck and onto his back, grabbed his horns and rode him for about an hour all over creation, jumping over rivers, fences, houses and mountains. It was a real kick in the butt.

"Back at the house, Ruth told how Murphy could easily satisfy 10 cows in heat. I leaned back on the sofa and boastfully said I could, too, since my heart surgery. My wife said the bull was getting too thick now. And Ruth, sensing I was in trouble, went for the kill. She said when one of her macho animals jumps a fence to re-arrange the neighbor's landscape, she gives him a 'visit to the freezer.' I wasn't sure what she meant until I saw my wife's cold stare.

"So doc, I'm excited that the buffalo is making a comeback. It's a healthy alternative to beef and they're more fun to play with than cows. And for saving my life, I brought you this gift to get rid of flies and pesky patients."

"What is it?"

"It's Murphy's tail, an appropriate end to my tall story."

Casting a Spell on Fishing Reality

Fishing and politics are similar.

I was as enthusiastic about the season's first fishing outing as Bill Clinton must have been when he first entered the White House.

All he has left on his political plate now is a skeleton, with the meat picked away by the reality of the job.

All I have left are memories of big fish I never caught.

Politicians use the bait of deceiving rhetoric to hook votes. Fishermen use lures and enticing food to get their prey.

Reality hurts.

It was a beautiful day in Seattle. My wife kissed my unshaven cheek and said, "Get the big one." I was on my way to Spokane. Armed with new equipment, an inflatable boat and a *fish assassin* baseball cap on my head, I took off for a new adventure.

I arrived four hours later and headed for the first lake. The little compressor worked and the giant, four-person inner-tube inflated perfectly. I jumped in, the tackle box jumped out. Fortunately, the water was shallow, so I was able to retrieve it quickly.

Two hours later I met Cory at an RV park. He had told me many fine fishing stories during our friendship.

"How did you do?" he asked. "Forget it, pal. Those fish have low self-esteem. The trout don't think they deserve the gourmet, garlic-flavored power bait I was offering them. The only bite I got was from a big mosquito."

Cory squirmed.

"Didn't you know you're not allowed to use bait in that lake, only lures. That's a bass lake."

"What's the difference? A fish is a fish," I said, relieved I wasn't snagged by the local ranger.

We left in the morning for Idaho where Cory said he'd heard fish are so hungry they "jump on the hook." We arrived at Coeur d'Alene and looked at the big lake.

"No way I'm getting in that raft in *this* place," I told him.

"Okay," he said. "Let's go to Missoula. I hear the trout are as big as rainbows there."

Never been to Montana, I thought. Why not?

We arrived in Missoula — steak country. I excitedly ordered one medium rare. It came to the table. It was like leather. The second came cold and raw in the middle. The third was just right.

We went to a bait store. "Where's the fish?" I asked.

"They're biting at the lake about 60 miles from here," said the clerk. "Better hurry, those storm clouds are about to burst."

My enthusiasm already had.

We returned to Couer d'Alene. We arrived at 5, went straight to the banks of the lake. I cast more than 100 times with the Sure Fire rooster tail lure Cory let me borrow. Nothing. It was getting dark.

"Let's go home. This sucks."

A sudden jerk on the line changed my mind. "I got one, I got one, get the net!"

I reeled it in. Cory stood by gallantly to assist.

We looked at each other with amazement. It's incredible how strong a 7-inch trout can be. We shook our heads and let it go.

I tried again, now in the dark, hoping to catch dinner. It was useless. Cory, as designated drinker, had finished his six-pack long ago and hunger was growing equally with our frustration.

We arrived in Spokane, disillusioned after the 450-mile trek. We had fish and chips for dinner.

In the morning I went solo to a small recreational lake near the RV park to contemplate life. I sat alone on the dock watching birds dive into the water and leave with mouthfuls of fish. I put the gourmet power bait on the hook and dropped it into the shallow water.

Incredibly, I caught two, 10-inch trout. They, too, had low self-esteem. What kinda fish would get caught by such an amateur?

Exhausted, I returned to the RV park. Cory gladly accepted the fish for dinner. I packed and prepared to go home.

"It's been fun, Cory. I guess I'll just keep watching those TV fishing documentaries until I get it right. Let's do this again and forget about catching fish. I'm as lucky with them as I was with women — guess I don't have the right bait."

Cory put his arm on my shoulder and quietly admitted he had never fished before, but had learned many good stories from local travelers. I smiled knowingly.

"Hey, we spent time together. We shared some good laughs, had a couple good meals and saw some new places. Not so bad."

I arrived home, tired and filthy.

"I got two in a trout pond, honey They weren't big, but Cory's enjoying them for dinner tonight. What's new in the news?"

"Well, no progress in Bosnia. The economic stimulus package is still limp. Health-care proposals are sick, and the recession is still depressin'. Same-o, same-o."

There's something fishy going on in this world. Whether you're a hopeful politician or a hopeful fisherman, you can't expect too much. Reality has a way of reeling you in. But it's fun trying.

Good luck Mr. Clinton.

Making Money With the Right Chemistry

I met investment counselor John Wong at a recent social gathering of important people. They were all there; insurance and real estate agents, dentists, plumbers and owners of the hair salons, hamburger joints, auto shops and pet stores. No politicians in sight.

I had sneaked in the back door, assimilating the latest O.J. chatter, when Mr. Wong approached me cautiously.

"Hi, I'm John Wong. How are you? Would you like to make lots of money? Here's my card. Call me."

I admire confidence. I gave him a dirty quarter. "Here. Make some money on this and we'll talk," I chuckled.

He called a week later. "Hi. John Wong here. I've got a dollar for you." Was he serious?

Copies of *Business Week, Money, Smart Money,* and *The Wall Street Journal* were in the waiting room. I shuffled through the stack and found *The National Enquirer, Cosmopolitan* and *Sports Illustrated.* I breathed easier seeing something familiar. He came out, shook my hand and put something in it.

"Here's the dollar we earned." There were four, shiny new quarters. "Now give me the deed to your house, your check book and the pink slip to your car. We'll make a bundle." I admire confidence.

"Whoa! How are you going to do that?"

39

"Well," he said, "*we're* going to buy some junk bonds, mutual funds, stocks and money-market funds — safe, sure and fast investments."

"Why should I trust you?"

"I have a degree in chemical engineering, 10 years of investment experience and own three cars, a large house and a big bank account."

"Oh? So why did you quit your job as a chemical engineer?"

"I was working to clean up the environment. It's more profitable to clean up in the financial world."

I began to like this guy. An honest man is hard to find.

"Well, listen, I'm no fool," I lied. "I know about junk bonds. I've got a bunch locked in boxes to sell at the next community garage sale. I know about mutual funds too. That's where a bunch of folks put their money together in a pool and then lose their shorts swimming with the sharks."

"Well, not exactly. Let me expla . . ."

"Why do you work for a company called Ed Jones? That's pretty tame. Doesn't do as much for me as those Merrill Pinch or Pain and Webbers companies. They sound more aggressive. Is your company related to the Down and Jones Industrial Company?"

"Well, no, not exactly. Our motto is 'Get big-time results for the small-time investor.'"

"Oh, now I get it. You think I'm small time, do you? Trying to take advantage? Well, I want you to know my grandfather left me with plenty of shares of stock in Howard Hughes Airlines and the Death Valley Water Works."

Mr. Wong raised his eyebrows, then went to the rest room. I took the opportunity to peek into the other room in the back.

He returned.

"Okay, Mr. Wong. Before I give you more money I want to know how you turned my quarter into a dollar?"

"Invested in a good stock. Pepsi. It was the right choice!"

"Got ya! I saw that chemical lab in the back. Now I know how you earn money the old fashioned way. You *make* it! That chemistry education sure helps, doesn't it? You chemically laundered my dirty quarter and made three more, didn't you? Now I know why investment counselors say, 'don't put all your eggs in one basket.' It's because they might crack. Your golden eggs are made of silver!"

I pointed to an electronic device on his desk. "Don't deny you're secretly tied in with those slick Wall Street insiders, while the rest of us suckers are left on the outside paying for your fortunes.

"I glanced through *Fortune* and didn't see your company listed. I'm not sure you're legit."

"But," Mr. Wong smiled, "We're connected with the *Psychic World Cable Network*. If you call 1-900-MONEY4U, you'll discover we're listed at the top of the Fortune Cookie 500."

I quickly left Mr. Wong's office.

At home, I proudly showed my wife the shiny quarters, bragging about my financial wisdom. I put them safely under the mattress with our $72 investment portfolio.

She frowned at me, pointing to Mr. Wong's picture in the local newspaper. The headline read *"Investor of Year Buys Dow Chemical Company, After Testing New Products in Home Lab."*

Mr. Wong turned down my dinner invitation. "I prefer junk bonds to junk food," he smiled politely.

Like I said, I admire confidence.

The Sky's a Weird Envelope

The Kite Man and Bubble Lady are local weirdoes. Their hobbies are strange compared to those enjoyed by the rest of us who are somewhat normal. I've seen them many times at the Mukilteo State Park along the water, while walking my tortoise on the rocks as others ate lunch, watched the boats and fed seagulls.

"Watch out!" said the man excitedly as his red and orange kite darted dangerously close overhead. "Me?" "Yes, you." I walked over to him cautiously.

"You should find something more interesting to do than walking a reptile!"

"Like what? Flying a kite?" I said facetiously.

"It's fun," he said, "watch this . . . the 'homesick angel.' " The kite shot up into the sun. "Here, you try it." I took one of the two strings, he held the other. The "homesick devil" dove straight to Hell.

"I'm sorry. I haven't been told to fly a kite for many years."

He smiled and picked up the fallen angel. "Don't worry, it's made of nylon and graphite. Let me show you some tricks." The kite darted straight up, cut quickly to the right, then straight down, left about five feet above the ground, and straight up again.

"That's amazing!" I said. "How did you do that?"

This was no ordinary weirdo. Tom was a former Air Force pilot. After his retirement he became a champion kite flyer. He was as charged up about his hobby as Ben Franklin must have been when he discovered electricity. My curiosity was sparked.

"Kites were used more than 3,000 years ago in China," he explained. "With glass on their edges, they were effective weapons in battle. They're still used in fishing to take bait far out over the water and drop it. On a battleship, they're used for target practice. Handled by experts, several can fly together in tandem, much like the Blue Angels. And they're good for upper body exercise."

"Exercise? Yeah, right," I said, disbelieving. He sent the four-and-a-half ounce, miniature hang-glider soaring back into the air. "Here, take both handles."

"No way!"

He insisted. Whaaam!!! The force pulled me over onto the ground. I joined a *very* homesick devil. Tom laughed. "You can get up to 100 pounds of pull on these *small* ones," he grinned.

Then another weirdo walked over with his flying Skynasauer.

"I see you're learning the sport. Don't get discouraged. It took me awhile, too." I shrugged.

"Why do *you* fly?" I asked.

"Well, my dirt bike is broken and my boat and plane are in the shop. I gotta do *something* on a sunny day, don't I?" Weird.

"How come you don't send paper messages up the lines?" I asked, remembering my childhood kite experience. No answer. The men smiled at each other, then began chasing each other's kites in an utterly majestic and graceful air battle. The kites went up and down in long, sweeping turns, then sideways and then — crash! They came down simultaneously.

"What happened?"

"The currents have edges, much like an envelope, and if you get outside, you fall." This must be where the term "pushing the envelope" came from. They pushed it.

Both kites zoomed straight up, stopped like stalled airplanes, (called "parking"), then came down slowly and carefully to hover over a car parked in the lot. It was an amazing sight. With precise control, they made the kites tap gently on the windshield until the driver jumped out screaming. "What are you doing?"

"You're in our wind envelope! Could you please move?"

I had seen it all.

"So you still think flying a kite is boring?" The wind was taken out of my sail.

"Not exactly, but how many hours can you stand here just tapping, fighting, diving, parking and searching for envelopes?"

"Probably about 12 hours a week. I don't think of anything while I'm flying. It's very relaxing. I listen to Wagner operas and fly to his music. It gives me a chance to get away from my wife while she does her thing. Elaine's a champion in her sport, too."

She was watching us. She smiled and called me over to join her, but I'd had too much for one day with these strange people. I left with my tortoise, watching Elaine create gigantic soap bubbles that floated gracefully up into the atmosphere.

I slowly walked my companion home, took a bubble bath and then went out to buy a kite. I needed a new envelope to push.

Clamoring to Compete With Cal

Cal Ripken, Jr. earns big bucks playing on baseball fields. He got a visit to the White House in recognition of his record-breaking job attendance. Meanwhile, George Lettuce Picker Sr., who receives a salary suitable for a blind bus driver, got only a handshake from the boss he had never met, after enduring 40 years in the farm fields.

Something's wrong here. Mr. Ripken does deserve credit. He never whimpers for time off because mosquitoes interfere with his swing, or because his dislocated jock strap makes it difficult to run. He's a good man and good ballplayer, but he's no Lou Gehrig.

Real heroes are the unseen common folk performing everyday miracles of durability. We need a special day like Mothers' Day to recognize them for their performances in enriching society through interesting and entertaining behavior.

Here are some memorable characters I've met who I'd nominate for recognition.

Harvey hasn't fallen off his barstool for 22 consecutive days, a monumental record for the hard-working town drunk. The dive hasn't even been raided for three consecutive months — another achievement, considering Harvey's father, an ex-bootlegger, owns the joint. These are *real* records.

Marlena Romanoski, a high school crush of mine, majoring in foreign language, steadfastly rejected 27 monthly invitations to my drama classes to hear me recite Shakespeare in Australian. She said she hadn't studied that language yet and wouldn't understand much. She graduated in spite of her stupidity. What endurance!

Roberto Sanchez, a college acquaintance, sustained the torture of eating Wheaties for 365 straight mornings. He participated in a promotional experiment to prove champions are what they eat — and he needed tuition money. After he lost 12 straight amateur boxing matches, the company added salsa to the cereal. He ate the stuff 365 more consecutive days, then knocked out his next 12 opponents in the first round. When the company refused to put his picture on the cereal box, he admitted publicly the promotion was flaky and said that he preferred Cheerios with his steroids. He graduated with honors. There's a hero!

Bob Outhouse, another high school classmate, was denied a new name by the U.S. Department of Corrections, after writing 200 letters requesting some relief. The committee chairman, Bill Peebody, determined he wasn't eligible for consideration because Bob refused to sign his full name on the 25-page government request forms. Bob appealed, writing 50 more letters with his full signature. He was granted a new name. Bob Petrie is now considering legal action. Talk about perseverance!

Lizzie Osborne, another old flame, burned out after 12 children (*not mine!*) but continues striving for sanity and respectability. She worked 487 straight days without error, stamping letters on metal plates in the assembly line. She was awarded two days off for outstanding work and good behavior and promoted to the vanity line where she created a personalized NOTGLTY license plate to take with her when she leaves. Lizzie still hopes for parole, knowing her stolen Ferrari mini-van is getting lonely awaiting its new plates. Now that's fortitude!

Nobody gave Ruggiero Fellini, a somewhat eccentric Italian painter, any hope of completing the stripe down Interstate 10 between Mobile, Alabama and Jacksonville, Florida. In spite of interruptions by State Police for working drunk in the dark and arguments over creative differences with Transportation Department planners about his colorful and artistic interpretations of the word "straight," Ruggiero still finished the project in 17 years. He didn't get paid for his efforts because he didn't follow the rules, but his effort and ego were rewarded by autograph seekers caught in the traffic jams created by the Fellini Line. A classic and hardy artist indeed!

Mary Evans, who owns a very special day-care kennel, managed to outlast Markie for two full weeks. He escaped from two pairs of cuffs, clawed his way out of three scuttle-ball cages, ate all the nutritional treats (*including the wrappers*), refused sanitary assistance on the slides and merry-go-round, broke four ropes and then drowned and decapitated an entire flotilla of Barbie Dolls in the plastic wading pool. Unaware that Mary's an experienced, liberated Sumo wrestler, Markie finally challenged her to mortal combat. Mary admitted later she might have been a bit harsh administering the *Evans' Crunch,* but "that chubby St. Bernard needed to learn it's over when the *fat lady* sits." Mary certainly earns my respect.

Now, even my wife is claiming a place in history. For putting up with me all these years, she's a champion deserving of equal recognition with Cal — and, according to her, equal pay.

Supermalls: If the Shoes Fit, Wear 'Em

Shopping is an adventure — I've never understood why.

So I accepted, with only mild enthusiasm, the press-preview invitation to the grand opening of the million-square-foot SuperMall of the Great Northwest.

The 155-acre spread was easy to find. The new freeway signs clearly marked the giant landmark. There isn't anything else to see or do in the city of Auburn, I suppose, so why not build a mall there to justify some new highway work?

The discount mega-mall will be a major tourist attraction, according to the disgraceful promotional materials, comparing expected visitor numbers to those for the Eiffel Tower, Empire State Building, the Seattle Space Needle and, when completed, the O.J. Simpson Memorial Crime Lab.

There are four theme entrances. I spotted the miniature replica of Mt. Rainier adorning the entrance I used. The other three were designated by a train, an airplane and a carousel. This is designed to help you find your car when you leave. But the real psychology, I figure, is if you buy lots of items, (*they estimate an average $200 per visit*), you exit first class through the airplane, if you spend a lesser amount, the train, and if you can afford to return and stretch your spending muscles, the mountain route. For those less fortunate, using the carousel entrance is a reminder that shopping without money to spend is a dizzying experience.

Even without much money to spend, my neurosis prevented me from riding the carousel. It had these speedy horses, an ostrich, a rooster — but no tortoises, snakes or slugs, so I entertained myself eating crayfish at the Cajun Grill instead.

At fast-food concessions, managers were desperately trying to orient their young chefs on the art of quickie cuisine. "No, they've never cooked before," said one boss. "But they have enthusiasm and state-of-the-art equipment to help them learn 'hands on.' " One, with his hand on the digital register, said proudly with a broad grin, "We know real good how to collect the money." Amen.

I entered the Hall of Expenditures, walking on highly-polished hardwood flooring. According to the publicity information, wood is easier on the legs of patrons, expected to spend from four to six hours shopping at a time. Sure. But I suspect it's just another marketing ploy — with eight shoe stores in the mall, what a great track to try out new athletic footwear for frantic shopping adventures.

At the Off Saks Fifth Avenue Outlet, I was told the merchandise was new, but had been cleared off the racks at the *real* store. I think this means it didn't sell at ridiculous prices or it looked better on a mannequin than it would on a real person, so it's on sale now at regular prices. Marketing. It's a phenomenon.

The promoters expect tourists to visit. Really! There are 25 parking spaces just for buses. July is the busiest tourist shopping month and there's usually *some* sunshine here at that time, so I guess the two sunglasses shops will survive. Most reasonable locals know there are only a limited number of sunshine days in the Great Northwest, and umbrellas are more protective than sunglasses. I think the two lingerie stores will do better — they're weather-proof.

As I walked past the Black Market Mineral Shop, the Perfumania store, the Walk the Dog pet store, Surf City Squeeze juice bar and the Country Clutter gift shop, I realized how difficult it must be to create a unique store name. It was comforting, however, to see the sign "rest room" and not find anything inside reminding me to buy something I don't need.

When I took my wife to the real grand opening the next day to share with her my new knowledge of the shopping experience, I was apprehensive about being able to pay our mortgage that month.

But the adventure didn't cost more than gas and food for the 100-mile trip, because my wife, bless her heart, only performed The Basic Shoe Routine. After searching the eight stores for the "right" shoe, she said disgruntled, "They don't have the right size, the right color or the right price."

Some things never change. Shoes don't fit my wife and the shopping adventure doesn't fit me. I can now appreciate the benefits of TV shopping a lot more.

Almost Everyone's a Celebrity at Town Festival

I poked my head out the window, awakened by strange noises nearby on this dreary Saturday morning. Reluctantly, I dressed and walked across the street to the church parking lot where all the commotion was coming from. I had forgotten about the annual Mukilteo Town Festival.

Assorted and noisy attractions were congregating. The usual performers were there: pets, kids, politicians, antique car owners, cheerleaders and a couple of horses. I wasn't invited to perform this year because the clown quota had been filled by more accommodating individuals willing to wear the traditional garb.

Town festivals are noteworthy because, other than garage sales, pancake breakfasts or car accidents, it's the only time neighbors see each other up close. I had to walk by some of them quickly, so I wouldn't be reminded of the borrowed books and tools I still had.

These annual events also offer opportunities for participants to achieve attention and fame. Our town isn't very large yet and, so far, nobody's revealed our underground, no-tax, black-market movie theater and shopping mall, so the network news crews never show up. But Paul, the publisher of our local paper, was lumbering about taking pictures of all the important events. I stopped by to say hello, but was disappointed by his refusal to shoot a picture of me for the front page of *The Beacon*. He reminded me I hadn't reached celebrity status yet. Notoriety, yes, but not yet celebrity.

The parade finally began, and I quickly picked up some of the hard candy and Tootsie Rolls thrown all over the streets for kids to stuff in their pockets. Getting into the spirit of the parade wasn't that difficult, although I don't think Mayor Sullivan appreciated the Tootsie Roll I tossed at him while he rode by as Grand Marshall. I stood in awe, watching several courageous kids speed down Hill Street in slick soapboxes emblazoned with stickers from Pennzoil, STP, Luigi's Pizza and the Miss Directed for City Council campaign.

I took a quick side trip to the Beer Garden, where I noticed City Council and Business Association members drinking morning samples. For once, they all took me seriously and agreed with every one of my economic and political views they had always rejected in the past. When I suggested *all* Council meetings take place on Saturday mornings at Harvey's tavern, they slapped me on the back for my excellent suggestion and poured me more complementary samples. I like respect!

After I wobbled back to the parade, I could better appreciate the march music leading the young paraders along the half-mile route. A man carrying the kids' portable stereo reassured me recorded music was better than having untrained musicians playing out of tune — it saved the youngsters from embarrassment. I disagree. As a youngster, I remember a second-week tuba student playing out of tune and being the highlight of the parade. He loved the attention. I never tried playing again, though.

The fire engines, police cars and emergency vehicles demonstrating their sirens, however, reminded me I didn't like noise that much, after all. The kids loved it. So did the singing dogs, it seemed, although my neighbors, who prefer watching Saturday TV sports in the privacy of their homes, were enraged when they got no response from 911 after reporting disturbances of the peace. All the cops were working the streets. When I walked past officers Smith and Jones, they grinned at me, a reminder of my tickets for parking in their personal "no parking" spaces at the station.

A crotchety old man, who is very attuned to noise, became the most memorable event for me at this year's Festival. He tunes pianos. After the event, he graciously came over to take a look at my keyboard. We spent most of the time exaggerating macho military stories about how we escaped from KP and guard duties. I made lunch and gave him good wine to encourage more of his outrageous stories. He told me he had come from Los Angeles to visit his son. "This was the best parade I've ever seen," he said.

"You can't mean that, can you?" I asked.

"Sure," he smiled. "It's my son Paul's favorite too. That's why I flew up here."

"You're kidding?"

"Nope. It was in his paper last year. Had to see for myself."

"Which paper?"

"Your local one, *The Beacon*. My son's the publisher."

Now, I'm guaranteed a front page celebrity photo next year. My new friend, this wonderful, funny old man, recommended it to his connection — but I still refuse to wear the traditional clown garb.

Massage Therapy Relaxes Marital Stress

I left Trisha's office in a peaceful, relaxed trance. Life was good, I thought — until I got home and had to explain.

"You what?"

My wife doesn't always appreciate my efforts to be a more relaxed and wonderful person. "It was just a massage, honey. You said I was getting intolerably crabby in spite of all those relaxation tapes and healthy-living books, so I wanted to try something else."

"I suppose you think a massage is the answer?"

"Don't know yet. Gotta let my body adjust to the treatment."

"And how long is that going to take?"

"Don't know yet."

"Well, for now you have to mow the lawn and fix the fence."

"Can't. I'm too relaxed. It would break the spell, and then I'd be cranky again."

She frowned disapproval. "Okay, so tell me what happened."

"Well, first she told me to take off my clothes and lay on the table, face down with my head in a little hole so I could breathe, and also, I think, so I couldn't see what she was doing. Left my shorts on though, so you wouldn't be jealous."

"Jealous of what?"

"Very little, I guess.

"Anyway, she started on the shoulders with some kinda greasy stuff and rubbed it in real good. It hurt in some places. I told her I probably work too hard taking out the trash and lifting all those heavy tree branches that fell in the yard.

"Then she worked on my back. She pressed so hard I could feel muscles pop. I told her I needed a sturdier recliner for watching TV. Then she did the legs. Said I had great calf and hamstring muscles. I told her it was because I played a lot of golf. But when she put my hands in warm, wet towels I jerked away quickly."

"Why?"

"Some of the guys in the Army thought it was funny to put some fellas' hands in warm water while they were sleeping. Made 'em wet their beds. I was getting so relaxed, I got worried."

"Geez. Then what?"

"Well, after the rub-down she fed me some herbal tea. Said it burns fat and improves mental clarity. I told her I'd prefer gin, but I drank the tea anyway. Didn't feel any different, but from then on I was able to understand her Holistic medicine jargon. Couldn't before. She said I'd live longer if I got my body in shape and got in touch with my spirits. But my gin wasn't nearby.

"When we were done, she gave me lots of water to flush out the toxins the massaged muscles had released. I told her I don't drink water except when I can't find gin. She could tell the mental affects of the tea were wearing off. I drank the water. Wasn't bad actually, until she put in some concentrated complex carbohydrates. I whined that I didn't like them in the water, so she gave me a dose in the form of candy. That wasn't bad at all — I saw her put the cap on the bottle — 'Energizer for Children.' I guess I was acting childish."

"You really did try to get some help. Good. Was she pretty?"

"Well, I don't remember, actually. My head was always in that hole, and when I turned over I was so relaxed I didn't want to open my eyes. She was friendly and gentle."

"Was she pretty?"

"She was really knowledgeable about nutrition, weight control and exercise. Had degrees and all that — has worked on more than 7,000 bodies, too. Even said I was one of the best bodies she'd ever seen. Twelve years in the business. Very capable."

"Very persuasive, too. Was she pretty?"

"Okay. Maybe so. But after all the work she did on me I was so calm and vulnerable the only thing I could think about was how beautiful you are."

"Uh, huh. And what did she recommend?"

"She has lotions for toning the body and removing cellulite. And pills to replace vegetables and improve athletic performance. And . . ."

"I hope you took that performance pill. Now that you're so relaxed and knowledgeable, you can give *me* a massage."

"Oh no, honey. Can't do that. I'm not licensed."

A few days later my wife came home late from shopping. "Sorry I'm late. I couldn't find what I wanted. I was very angry, so I got a massage from Jacques. He's very talented. I'm not crabby anymore. Life is good."

"Is he a hunk?"

Searching for Security in All the Wrong Places

We recently had a neighborhood crime-watch, block party.

This is where you *watch* to see who has the courage to eat your pot-luck goodies and hear the cop explain how *blockheads* can steal your property if you're not careful.

I hope officer Berg isn't still mad at me for borrowing the shotgun from his unlocked patrol car while he was talking. I just wanted to prove I knew something about crime, too.

The usual questions were asked. "If a burglar's in my house do I shoot to kill, just wing 'em, or encourage him to take my wife's China, jewelry and silverware, so I can buy a fishing boat with the insurance money?" "Is it legal to put poison in my garden to rid the neighborhood of strange pets?" "If I call 911 on a Saturday night and get a busy signal, does it mean I can go next door and bash the loud stereo myself?" "Is it legal to hang teenagers from a tree if they *hang out* in my yard?"

I was glad to meet these good neighbors. I never see them except when they emerge to watch the emergency vehicles — police cars, ambulances and tow trucks. I'm a paranoid escapee from crime-ridden Los Angeles, so I wasn't sure if they might not be experienced criminals getting to know prospective targets. I didn't let my dessert plate out of sight, nor did I tell anyone I hadn't fed my pet boa constrictor for several days.

When I returned to the party after hiding Berg's shotgun under my slimy friend's cage where my wife wouldn't find it, there was plenty of story-swapping going on among the amateur crime-busters. I heard lots of ideas I could use should I turn to crime-prevention or crime when my writing career fizzles. I stole a few to share with you.

"This low-life was going to hook up his four-by-four to my boat out back. It was two in the morning. I heard the clanking sound of the trailer hitch. I was ready to call 911, but laughed when I saw that my own, cheap anti-theft device had worked. That rotten, smelly catfish I left in the boat tank was very effective. You should've seen that thief high-tail it outa there!"

"My wife and I disagreed about the causes of violence in America. She got so angry she threw a shoe at me and broke a window. Then I threw my shoe at her and broke my golf trophy. Then I got *really* mad and rolled my bowling ball at her and the front door got smashed. Then she threw beer bottles at me and I cut my bare feet. I made it to the phone. When the officer arrived I explained how she had assaulted me. I told him she was a lousy mother, a worse cook, politically ignorant, drove a car like a teenager and was uglier than he was. He arrested me for verbal abuse. When I got out of the slammer, rehabilitated, I finally agreed with my wife that domestic violence is intolerable. Then I finished trashing the house."

"The other night I caught four suspicious characters appraising my new Corvette. I decided to be bold and try to talk the problem away, so I asked what they were doing. One of them, *more* boldly, advised me they were taking my car for an evening of joy-riding. When I pointed out it was only a two-seater, they thanked me and began looking over the neighbor's Cadillac. I told them the Caddy only got 9 miles a gallon. They counted all the money in their pockets and frowned. I pointed at the Honda down the street, but they were impatient. Fortunately, when the officer arrived, I was able to provide accurate descriptions of my watch, purse and diamond necklace."

I left the party early without hearing any more crime stories. When I got home there were two squad cars and an animal control vehicle out front.

I still don't know who tipped officer Berg about my slimy security pet. I'll bet it was that brat down the street who watches me catch rats with a fish net on Saturday nights. He was at the party, too. Reluctantly, I paid the $250 fine and said good-bye to Boa Boy.

Officer Berg offered me his sympathy when I returned his weapon. I smiled with generous appreciation when he handed me the newest police brochure on home security procedures. I still think I know a lot about crime prevention.

The next day I fed the brochure to my new pet alligator.

PART TWO:
Anecdotes of the Human Condition

Jurassic Park Brings Reality Into Focus

Steven Spielberg illustrates, once again, one of our most basic fears — being victimized by natural predators other than ourselves.

He's banked a bundle on this dreadful thought.

First in *Jaws* and now with *Jurassic Park*, this terrifying idea has reared its ugly head on the bodies of fascinating dinosaurs.

"That was awful," I overheard two elderly ladies say, as I walked out of the crowded movie theater. "Can you imagine those disgusting animals eating people and making piles of poop all over?"

I thought step-son Cory would enjoy the fantasy, but he, too, was disappointed.

"They were *bad*," he said. "They ate people and were mean."

It wasn't easy trying to explain they only did what they were supposed to do.

"They were predators," I said. "They ate meat. If they existed today, we'd be hunted all the time. They needed lots of protein to survive. They were *always* hungry, just like teen-agers and sharks. And they had the same bad manners, always leaving behind big messes wherever they went."

"Yuk."

Unintentionally, I'm sure, Spielberg stimulated some deep, dark inner thoughts most of us prefer to deny — we often behave more like sharks and dinosaurs than the kind, considerate and thoughtful animals we'd like to believe we are.

Watch people eat. Knives slash slabs of beef, chicken or fish on the plate. The catch is then brutally pierced with a pronged device and hoisted gracefully (*by some*) into the mouth.

It's then systematically chewed and swallowed, a most disgusting process if you look closely — just as the stars of *Jurassic Park* so vividly demonstrated. No wonder Mom always told us never to talk with our mouths full.

Yes, we *are* like those dinosaurs, like it or not. The difference between us and the rest of the animal world, is we *think* we're more *intelligent* — that's why we're willing to pay $50 for a football game rather than get flu shots — more *considerate* — like drug lords who provide an easy way out. *kinder* — like Hitler, who only wanted to make his country prosper — and more *compassionate* — like Saddam Hussein, who kills people to make his country safer.

At the very least, dinosaurs behaved as they were intended to — they knew no other way.

What would *we* do if grocery stores were looted and destroyed? How many of us know how to hunt and fish to survive without someone else neatly packaging our prey in cellophane?

Do steers, chickens, fish and sheep look at us as mean and awful? Okay, Cory, can you see what I mean?

As *civilized* predators, most of us can control these instincts. We protect territory at work by adeptly "playing the game," and observing the proper "pecking orders." We defend our homes and yards as personal sanctuaries. Beware any intruders stepping over the boundaries to destroy or steal our property.

Primal behavior is demonstrated by those who "hunt" with credit cards, "Collecting goods for the lean times and keeping the nest comfortable," explains my wife. And it's the man's job, she tries to convince me, to "hunt" for a job. (*I somewhat agree, but being a house-bound writer, I find a "job" disturbingly disagreeable*).

I found humor in *Jurassic Park*. If dinosaurs can be re-created and put in a natural zoo-like setting to be observed, maybe aliens are watching *us* too, as we kill each other like dinosaurs.

Maybe someday, when humans are extinct, these same aliens will have to search for other life forms to amuse themselves. "To boldly go where no one has gone before."

Spielberg brought back the dinosaurs so we could go where no one has gone before. Millions of us were willing to spend money for the chance to see ourselves as prey, rather than the dominant hunters we think ourselves to be.

I had to tell Cory that unfortunately there are some people who kill for no reason other than power. There are also bad business people who take advantage of weaker victims. The dinosaurs did what they *had* to do. They, unlike humans, knew nothing else.

The silent lambs who watch simply and indignantly as Spielberg's "awful, disgusting animals" leave "big piles of poop" in their wake, should look at their own world again.

Our own behavior creates environmental waste and promotes predatory killing and political gridlock similar to the reality of Spielberg's entertaining fantasy.

The dinosaur was supreme in its time, too. It became extinct.

It's something to think about.

Conquistadors Revive Sleepy Souls

Pablo Pizorno can't be found in any history book, nor is it likely a marble replica of his magnificent torso (*his own perception*) will be displayed in his hometown of Vigo, Spain. But it's appropriate to immortalize him here for enhancing my life and for his contributions to diplomatic relations.

He and several of his Conquistadors Teenagers invaded our little town this summer as participants in an international student cultural program. They quickly conquered the language and timidity barriers, then proceeded to round up their spoils — baseball hats, CDs, designer T-shirts, sunglasses and all the hamburger and pizza they could gobble up in five minutes.

ADVENTURES IN THE SLOW LANE

Our own house guest, Pablo, was shy at first, and intimidated by the new experience — for about 20 minutes! Then he quickly caught on to me.

I showed the 17-year-old his own room, then took him on the one-minute tour of our estate — bathroom, telephone, refrigerator and TV. "Where Sega?" he asked. I showed him, then held out my hand, but he didn't offer a tip. As well as I could, I explained it's the American way to pay for good service. "Thank you, no" he said politely, refusing any more of my hospitality. My wife warned me about further improprieties.

Pablo was sweating like an over-worked arena bull the next day. "What have you done?" screamed my wife. "Well," I said innocently, pointing to the lawn, "he likes mechanical things — wants to be an engineer — so I taught him how to use the power mower."

We went to Seattle. Pablo pointed excitedly at a large bull painted on the store front of the Cowchip Factory. "Toro!" It was another opportunity I couldn't miss. I translated, using gestures inappropriate to describe here, what a cowchip was and that they were imported from Texas. "Taste gusto," I told him. "Gracias, no gracias." As I dragged him into the store, he pleaded, "No, please. No like. Thank you. Please, no." I bought a big one. When my wife took a bite and smiled, Pablo turned red, then a little green. Like a brave matador, he took the plunge and enjoyed the chocolate-chip cookie. He grinned. "You make joke."

Modern conquistadors don't ride white horses or wear armor anymore. I was disappointed. Now they ride motorcycles, wear painted T-shirts, listen to rock music on portable CD players and eat donuts and pizza. So we spent the next day visiting three motorcycle shops, two donut shops, four music stores and counted 12 pizza parlors around town. "I like," was Pablo's favorite phrase, as he observed what America has to offer.

His most excited "I like," was at the Harley Davidson shop where he dressed up in biker garb. He looked pretty silly covered in black leather. So I took the souvenir photo reluctantly, warning him that sitting on a Harley holding a beer can, smoking a cigarette with a macho sneer and having a curvaceous young woman (chica, *in Spanish*) standing beside him, would certainly give his friends back home the wrong impression of America. I was afraid too, that his parents might not approve of this educational experience.

I took another photo of him on the bike dressed in his regular garb. He looked even sillier now. I advised him. "You're an honor student." But he said, "I no student now. Today I am 'easy rider.'" What an influence our movies have on foreigners!

The next day he, along with his other comrades, became *fashionable*. I once again gave in to his wishes. I helped him dye his hair blue. "Now I rock star." The weird sunglasses didn't enhance his disguise much. But, he was *cool*!

Pablo knew Seve Ballesteros was a famous Spanish golfer, so he was delighted to go golfing with my wife and me. "I be good caddie," he said. After five holes searching for my errant shots in the bushes, he asked politely, "Only four more?" His face turned gloomy when I grinned and said, "Thirteen more." I offered him $10 for another round. "Gracias, no." I offered $25. "Try another people, okay?" I've never been very lucky when it comes to buying respect.

I learned more from Pablo than he did from me. He was unusually courteous and a wonderfully slick liar. He ate everything I cooked, mowed the lawn and walked our dog, always with an, "I like." He knew more about American music and history than I. And he was more suave with *chicas* than I'll ever be.

The Conquistadors captured our hearts with their adventurous spirit, good humor and intelligence. Except for golf and being awakened before noon every day, I think Pablo enjoyed himself. For sure, he enriched our lives and awakened our sleepy souls.

The Faster We Go, the Further Behind We Get

Oil companies and fast-food chains are now building enlarged convenience stations where you gas up your car at the service pumps and gas yourself up at Burger King or McDonald's.

Where are we headed? Instead of stopping to smell flowers, we're sitting in our cars smelling exhaust fumes. Technology makes our lives easier, yet emptier. It seems the faster we go, the further behind we get in learning the meaning of life. The only time for reflection we have these days is in front of TV and computer screens. We spend the saved time doing more things faster so we have more time to do more things — what's the point?

We're getting more convenience centers. *Stop* and *Shop*. *Stop* in with the kids, deposit them in Burger King's playground, *shop* 'til you drop. I can see it now . . .

I have just pulled into a tunnel. My car has been hooked underneath by one of several chain-driven conveyer belts.

"Welcome to the Stop & Shop Efficiency Tunnel. Please press your preferences on the control panel."

I reach out the window and punch in: Egg McMuffin for breakfast; Pizza Hut pizza for lunch. Then I push a button for full-service and the movie *Clear and Present Danger*.

"Here's your order sir." The car is pulled along through the wash (*my video-movie is playing on the VCR while I eat*) to the next station. The car is hoisted up and two mechanics quickly change the oil, put air in the tires and fill the tank with gas.

An H&R Block station was conveniently located at the mall entrance, so an hour later, when my computer-compressed video is over, I open the window and a clerk says, "Sir, please sign at the bottom and we'll mail your tax return to your home by the weekend."

The conveyor belt slowly pulls me by 96 store-fronts, where I pick up the boxes with new shoes, socks, tie, underwear, comic books, earrings and a copy of *Modern Shopper*, all of which I ordered on my home TV-computer the night before. It's time for lunch, and my pizza is handed to me through the window at precisely the right time.

I now pass through the music and video tunnel, where I see and hear excerpts from the latest movies and hit songs on the wall screens. I can order any of them by pushing buttons on the control panel at the end of the tunnel. Then, as I emerge from the tunnel, I pick up the laundry I left at the entrance.

It's early afternoon. I push a coded button on another control panel, and it buzzes the micro-receivers taped on the shoulders of my three kids, who are playing at the amusement park. It's time to meet me at Central Dispatch. They come running and jump into the car with happy faces.

Their glee is short-lived. The conveyer stops, and three white-coated ladies take the kids behind the shop front with a big red cross on it. *Mini-Medical*, the sign reads. The kids return 30-minutes later with clean teeth and all their back-to-school shots. I use the time getting my eyes tested for disposable contact lenses.

We're entering the final stages of the journey. The car goes through the ultra-sound check for scratches and internal mechanical malfunctions and is waxed by microwaves and robotic buffers.

We pick up the groceries ordered from home and receive our free bouquet of flowers and bonus coupons for spending more than $400. I pay the bill by flashing my personalized, coded laser beam flashlight into the credit panel at the end of the tunnel.

Something stinks here. It seems we're on the wrong track. This high-tech, fast lane stuff seems to be leading us away from the *quality time* I thought was important. The scent of roses should be favored over exhaust fumes — even if it means washing your own car and cooking your own food.

Education Needs Some Comic Relief

Some educated friends say I don't know very much because I don't read. I can't argue intelligently with them on most subjects, because they *do* read and have more facts to deal with.

I think too much knowledge sometimes complicates common sense and ruins the joy and innocence of ignorance. We need comic books and cartoons as universal tools to provide comic relief and education at the same time.

One educated friend recently pontificated on the rationale for America's involvement in the trouble spots of the world. He explained the historical background of the areas and the economic and social ramifications of the conflicts. I grasped his detailed explanations about as well as I did a greased pig at a Texas rodeo when I was younger.

I learned my basic economic concepts from Uncle Scrooge. Family behavior was well documented by the Flintstones. Superman and the Lone Ranger were inspirational role models for patriotism and the search for justice.

Winnie the Pooh and the tortoise didn't care that the owl was wiser or the rabbit faster. They left legacies of simple wisdom.

My adolescence was a difficult time, but Archie and his friends produced some swell answers for my teenage dilemmas. And for all his bumbling conflicts with Mr. Wilson, Dennis the Menace taught us about love and tolerance.

Batman and Robin solved problems through boffo teamwork.

I can't forget Popeye, who taught the benefits of healthy eating, in contrast to his friend Wimpy, the original fast-food junkie. Popeye also exemplified chivalry, protecting the honor of his true love, Olive, against the amorous intrusions of Bluto the Bully.

Tom and Jerry were examples of surviving in the jungle of life, using wit and cleverness. Mickey and Minnie were fine role models for loving relationships, and Tweety Bird exemplified peaceful co-existence, chirping cheerfully away while Sylvester attempted to turn off his music.

Porky Pig didn't let his not-so-perfect b-b-b-body interfere with basic wisdom. He accepted himself as he was, without allowing fad diets and health spas to interfere with the random thoughts within his alleged mind.

A foundation of common sense evolves from cartoon characters. Politicians and military commanders could stand on it if they weren't so caught up in their private, intellectual ego wars. At times, too much knowledge can interfere with simple solutions. For all their pontificating and analyses, politicians might be better off putting away their reports, books, speeches and statistics and reviewing the comics. Life isn't that complicated.

My step-son Cory and his friend Russ, both 12, achieve academic success in school. But they still love cartoons.

"CNN is boring," said Russ. "Lousy music comes on, and all you hear is bad news. I like to be happy, not sad."

Cory agreed. "Cartoons teach about real life, and they have good music. The Simpsons teach you how to be rude and make people laugh. The Mutant Turtles teach you how to protect people from bad guys, and they don't kill anybody. I also learn about famous artists like Michelangelo and Donatello."

"Buster and Babs are funny rabbits on *Tiny Toons*, said Russ. "They go to ACME college where they learn to make stupid faces and drop anvils on enemies without really hurting them. They make me feel good after listening to boring lectures about life from my dad and teachers."

"I think cartoons should replace weathermen," said Cory. "All they do is make funny faces and stupid jokes. Who cares? I'd rather watch Bugs Bunny do the weather. He would just say, 'That's all folks,' and then I could watch more cartoons."

"My favorite is Furball on *Tiny Toons*," said Russ. "He's a little cat who lives in a cardboard box and is always being bullied by big, mean cats. I learn how it must feel to be homeless, so I take real good care of my real cat."

I thought about what the kids said.

65

Daffy Duck could waddle down the aisles of Congress speaking his garbled dialogue with other politicians and make about as much sense. At least it would be funny, not sad.

"Cory, can I watch cartoons with you for awhile?"

He was delighted I was willing to learn about life *his* way. No lectures, no admonishments, just laughter.

In an Unfair World; Birth Is Punishment Enough

An American teenager visiting Singapore got a serious spanking for using spray paint to inflict heinous decorations upon innocent and defenseless cars.

The backlash of this act of adolescent misbehavior further demonstrates the unfairness of the world we live in. Crimes and punishments are too often determined by those guilty of their own misguided righteousness. Justice, like beauty, is always in the eye of the beholder. Not everyone has good eyesight.

I was the most beautiful baby ever born, for example. Through the eyes of my confused mother that first day, this was probably true. She wouldn't say that today, I can assure you.

So why did the doctor punish me with a swift slap on my sweet and tender cheeks?

If I remember correctly, I worked hard to squeeze my way out, although that imbecile cord, or whatever they call that thing, was one helluva mess to get untangled from. I guess I wasn't *that* excited about leaving my nine-month, personal-growth period in that quiet, secure world where responsibilities and transportation needs hadn't yet been conceived in my delicate and empty mind. But a spanking?

Even more punishment was inflicted when I was put into a crowded room with loud-mouthed brats I had little in common with. Instead of pizza and a cold beer, I was forced to drink milk — hardly an inspirational way to start life.

And what did this most beautiful baby get for putting up with these indignations? Another whack on the butt!

So much for fair punishment.

Killing people is punishable by death in most places. But if you're a dictator, a religious terrorist with an attitude, an expert video game manipulator, football player or muscle-bound, martial-arts expert with a movie contract, you're a hero instead, eligible for martyrdom, stardom and free bonus games.

If you defraud your insurance company by intentionally leaving the keys in your beat-up old car and park it in the middle of a vacant lot, you're okay; but the dumb thief who steals it gets locked up and doesn't even get to keep the keys.

Invasion of privacy is a serious offense; but if you interrupt an intelligent man reading the sports page in the bathroom, it's just plain, stinking offensive.

When you tell your kid to turn off MTV and clean up his room and he doesn't, you punish him by making him watch obnoxious adult sitcoms in *your* messy living room.

Hard-working, normal folks are punished for lacking talent; forced to pay high prices to watch entertainers who live like kings.

Political and corporate criminals can make millions selling books while many innocent, peaceful citizens don't have an opportunity to learn to read.

The *shot heard 'round the world* heralded the beginning of a new country where freedom and justice were to reign supreme. Yet Paul Revere raced through towns without getting a speeding ticket.

The American teenager in Singapore, whose *spanking heard 'round the world* provoked much thought about crime and punishment, might be wondering if he was spanked when he was born. If he wasn't, maybe he'll consider his teenage spanking retroactive punishment.

Justice is in the eye of the beholder.

Suing for Profit and Vengeance

Suing for profit has become a disgusting national past-time. It does, however, create career opportunities for those who are comfortable in briefs and don't want to work for a living. I'd like to try it sometime!

I'd also like to see the courts employ professional jurors. They would be the frail, the poor, the unemployable — a jury of *my* peers. They would be full-time court-sitters, working their butts off on the planks of justice, apportioning financial rewards to those shallow souls who blame everyone but themselves for their plights. Those who do real work could continue working without interruption.

Not a bad idea, huh?

In any case, a clever citizen who knows his rights and conscientiously believes he is a victim can make a good living in court. No jest.

If you're smart, you too could become a professional *suer*, going after those who have made your life miserable — and make good money while avenging the wrong-doings of those in your past.

Forget the statute of limitations. Only the lack of creativity can limit your opportunities. Here are examples of how I could become a profitable legal professional without attending law school. A *suer*, if you get the drift.

I'll sue Mrs. Hancock, an otherwise wonderful eighth-grade math teacher, for whacking my butt with her famous Fanny Paddle, just because I scored a direct hit on her with a spit-wad and won a 25-cent classroom bet. Child abuse, you know.

I'm going to sue my high-school journalism teacher, Mr. Barraca, for making me re-write a sports editorial. I had chastised our football coach because an embarrassed John Outhouse was prevented from having his nickname, Jungle John, used in the football program. Instead, I was forced to write that John shouldn't be allowed to play football until he changed his name. Free speech, you know.

And certainly, I'm going after that apathetic judge who married me to my first wife. He sat there emotionless as she screamed, "No, no, no, let me go, let me go," while I pushed her into his office. I suffered for three long years for my immature blunder. Social malpractice, I think.

I'm going after the company that makes Wheaties. I'm still no champion, and I had to quit eating breakfast on doctor's orders — I was getting too flaky. False and confusing advertising.

If I can ever find Melinda, an old girlfriend I met in New York, I'll sue her for causing my low self-esteem. She said she loved me for who I was. But when she found out that I wasn't who I said I was because I wasn't sure I was who I thought I was, she left me twisted in emotional agony on the street for another man who didn't know who *he* was either — but had a job. Emotional cruelty.

I'm going after Warren, a former friend and colleague, for lying to our boss that *he* creatively worked our expense accounts into the personal profits we used to buy our yacht. *I* did the cheating, yet *he* got the recognition as a financial genius and the promotion to vice president of corporate finance. *I* got fired. Lack of character, I think.

Old friend David Silver will surely be surprised when he gets his subpoena. I quit my high-paying job to write, and now *he's got* my job! So, I'm suing him for lying to me eight years ago about how writing a column is an easy way to get rich. I believed him because he said he was always right! Immoral ethics, I think.

If this suing trend continues, somebody will charge God in a class action suit for creating human stupidity. He'd probably get an acquittal, though, because none of those professional jurors would risk His wrath and face unemployment again.

It's something to think about — unless you're a lawyer.

To Be Thankful and Not a Turkey

Thanksgiving was the first big celebration of a good harvest.

Fortunately, the conservative doctors and dietitians of the day were holed up somewhere concocting healthy reasons for not participating in the festivities. This was good, because the enthusiastic Pilgrims had more food, tobacco and alcohol to enjoy. They knew how to celebrate life and let tomorrow be damned.

It's good to be politically correct on this special day. If you can't see images any sharper than the wipers on your windshield, don't drive. If you smoke, go outdoors and throw the butts in storm drains when no one is looking. And if you eat too much, ask politely if anyone needs to use the bathroom before you do. I wouldn't suggest that anyone should eat, drink or smoke in excess. But for one day, it's nice to be thankful you have friends and family who allow you to do so without feeling guilty or ashamed.

I've always enjoyed Thanksgiving. Perhaps this year more than others, because it's an election year — good for calorie-burning arguments with the family over which turkeys, the Republicans or the Democrats, will make our holiday meal cost more next year.

But there are other important reasons to be thankful.

My neighbor learned to secure the lid on his trash can, so I don't have to rake his garbage off my lawn. I'm also thankful he sold his house and moved before I backed into his garage.

I'm thankful the tax auditor had to take remedial math after graduating from the IRS Academy and was, therefore, more sympathetic to my inept accounting practices. He was a good sport and helped me correct my errors. I'm still wondering, however, how I'm going to pay for his leniency and put his two children through college so I can avoid criminal charges.

I'm grateful to our mayor for agreeing to work within the budget after voters turned down funding for the library, park and paramedics He should be lauded for his sense of civic responsibility. He eliminated cheese from the menu at his pizza parlor to help prevent heart attacks, so we would need fewer emergency medical

70

services. He's also offering grateful citizens five free glasses of beer if they pay for the first three. Who needs to read or walk in a park after enjoying this generous hospitality?

I'm thankful to still be nimble and childish enough to beat most of the neighborhood kids at Mortal Kombat, the video game. And my wardrobe is still in style, too. Baggy and wrinkled pants and extra-large shirts have always been my favorite fashion. I can proudly say I still wear some I've had since my first childhood.

I'm thankful TV talk shows have demystified programs like *Father Knows Best, Leave It To Beaver* and *Lassie,* by revealing what was happening behind closed doors all those years. Montel, Oprah, Phil and others finally brought out the truth. I'm thankful to know now that bald men married to overweight women are 20 percent happier than pregnant women who marry their lovers' best friends before the child is born.

I'm thankful to Geraldo to know that if you're on a blind date, chances are you will: *1)* like the person; *2)* hate the person; *3)* marry his or her brother, sister, mother, or ex; *4)* get lucky or be sued for physical abuse; or *5)* decide to stay single.

And I'm *very* thankful no one has any *really good reasons* not to gobble up all you can on Thanksgiving Day.

Unless you're a turkey, you have a lot to be thankful for.

Wine Is Fine If You Have the Time

I always thought it would be fun to be an intellectual snob or sophisticated elitist. It's probably my envy of all the famous entertainers, generals, business tycoons, presidents, dictators, newspaper publishers and other powerful and imaginary friends of mine. They get to eat at good restaurants that have salt and pepper shakers and catsup bottles that don't plug up and eat with forks that don't bend if you bite on them too hard.

ADVENTURES IN THE SLOW LANE

I've always felt uncomfortable at fancy parties where beers with names I can't pronounce are served in pilsner glasses instead of cans and bottles, and the beans and ribs are served on ceramic plates instead of paper. Those are the parties where I frequently leave early, usually at the host's request.

So I told my wife, "We need to get some culture."

"Why?"

"I don't know. It's something different."

I've always heard wine is the drink of gods and cultured people, so we went to a wine-tasting party at the nearby winery.

There were at least two hundred people there. The tables had cloth on them instead of vinyl. Six half-filled glasses of wine and some kind of weird-looking food were in front of each of us. I looked under the table for the jug, but couldn't find one. I got an elbow in the ribs from my wife. Others at the table looked at me with strange expressions on their dour faces.

We smiled and nodded our heads a lot without saying much to the sophisticated strangers, except when I mentioned the weather hadn't changed since weather began, but nobody got the joke.

The winemaker announced pompously that the wines on our table were *reserved limited bottlings.* "I guess that means they save them just for these parties because nobody can afford them," I said laughing. The others glared at me again.

The winemaker went on and on, belaboring the description of how the 1980 Cabernet Sauvignon was made from grapes grown in sandy ground, because then the skins and seeds ferment better while they float around in oak barrels for a few months and then the tannin has a longer after-taste; unless, of course, the grapes have no taste at all, because they were picked when it was raining and were rotten. Well, it went *something* like that. I was about to take the first sip of the stuff when my wife asked for a straw. Since we didn't see any at the table, I figured that was inappropriate, so I said to her we should copy the behavior of the learned people sitting with us.

First, you swirl the stuff in the glass. This is to see if there is any loose dirt, bits of raisins or bugs in the stuff, I thought. But I

72

learned it's really to check the wine's body and sugar content. If, for example, the wine makes lots of streaks with no evidence of hair on the side of the glass, it has great *legs*. This is good because then there is *body*, although I couldn't see any anatomical parts floating around.

Then if it fits, you stuff your nose deeply into the glass and inhale the alcohol. This isn't to get high for courage to taste the stuff. I learned it was really to sniff the berry, oak, tobacco and other pleasant aromas good red wines produce. I couldn't detect anything except the familiar smell of alcohol, so I chugged the fruit juice in two swallows. This was a mistake. I coughed and choked loudly, embarrassing myself, my wife and the others at the table. The red stains on my denim shirt are reminders of the evening.

Unlike beer, wine is supposed to have a nasty, bitter taste that makes you pucker up. So if I puckered too much, I did what all the others were doing and spit out what I could muster into the cups on the table. I was pretty good at this part, although I thought it was unusual behavior for snobs. A plain-clothes cop that was part of the group noticed after awhile that I swallowed more than I spit and escorted me out to my car for a necessary little rest.

That was impressive! I felt safer and smarter knowing he was there. When you're sophisticated, you get treated better. If you drink too much beer or whiskey at a tavern, you get escorted to another place not known for its hospitality or comfort.

We had a good time getting cultured. We learned that wine is the drink of choice for sophisticated people because they can afford to buy one bottle of good wine for the same price as a case of beer and a bag of pretzels. We figured that's because they can pay for good food in their stomachs and don't have room for all that beer.

We can't afford to sip and spit expensive wine, so we've accepted our fate as commoners, continuing to chew gum instead.

New Hope for Sufferers of "Shoppers' Shock"

It shall be written: *Article 5, Section C, Sub-directory 13.*

"Any person subjected against his will to prolonged or frequent exposure to Christmas shopping will hereby, upon being certified as suffering from chronic Shoppers' Shock, be excused from jury duty, sales tax and parking tickets for a period of one year.

Cities should adopt this new ordinance quick. Real quick, like before *The Rush*. Like hurry, please!

I first discovered I was suffering from this malady during a recent binge. We didn't buy anything, as usual, because *The Rush* was still 15 days away. Too early, according to my wife, to enjoy it. Sick!

When we returned home, my neck ached from jerking side-to-side avoiding frenzied shoppers and from looking up at price tags and then down at the miniature screen on my little computer that keeps track of prices. My stomach and I were upset because I lunched on two tired hot dogs with tainted onions and missed the championship basketball game on TV.

Still shaking from the run-in with the sales clerk at the mall who accidentally rang up $48 for a pair socks I almost bought, I spilled a glass of wine on the remote and had to call a TV repairman.

He charged extra. "I'm missing Christmas shopping with my family and losing sales commissions from my other job selling TVs at the appliance store," he explained. I thought he looked familiar.

I turned on the set and began to relax. I clicked onto one of those shopping channels. "Honey, I found a solution. Why don't we shop here? No parking, no hassles, no people, no noise and everything is clearly priced."

There was a long silence, raised eyebrows and a frown thrown in for good measure. "Would you still like those new golf clubs?" Back to the mall.

The next day was exciting. The mud on the windshield and icy roads made driving an adventure. I held my temper when the maniac in the parking lot backed into my car door. "Sorry, buddy. I was in a hurry. The sale at JoBob's Hardware ends in two hours."

"Not to worry, everything is beautiful. Happy holidays."

My wife was amazed. "That was a wonderful gesture of Christmas spirit, darling." I forced a smile.

The mall was crowded. Two teenagers wearing unlaced athletic shoes stumbled into me during their game of *tag* or whatever it is they do. As my hot dog hit the floor, I smiled at the mustard-stained kids. "Having fun? Great!"

I waited patiently outside as my wife browsed in the department store. I found something important to do. I made it to the front of the line just before she returned. I got my $15 instant autographed photo with Santa Claus — actually it was Mrs. Claus. But the former Miss America contestant didn't fool me or any of the other fellas who made wishes they knew she'd never fulfill.

I continued behaving admirably. After waiting patiently for 20 minutes while my wife purchased two Christmas cards, it was off to the golf store.

My new attitude worked. I swung every club — can't be too careful when you have a handicap high enough for that *Guinness* book. I bought the best.

On the way home, we stopped at the drug store for Christmas decorations. It took an hour. Now I was in the Christmas spirit!

We returned to the car and discovered my *new* clubs were now *used* — they belonged to someone else. So did the stereo, radar detector and our CDs. I screamed in agony. "*Shoppers' Shock.*"

I could never serve on jury duty. How could I be impartial to shoplifters or scumbag burglars? I need help. I've spent every dime I had, supporting the local economy. I have none left for taxes. Except for handicap spaces, I couldn't find decent parking. And without them I wouldn't have spent any money at all, so I shouldn't have to pay for the parking tickets.

I hope the City Council understands my plight and adopts the ordinance quickly. Like before *The Rush*. Like hurry, please!

Pride of Ownership: When It Rains, It Pours

Morris handed me a huge bill for his work. I went through the roof. "You've gotta be kidding!"

"Nope. Now you know what it means to save for a rainy day," he smiled. He took my money without a trace of sympathy, but consoled me with a reminder that the new roof was guaranteed for 25 years — excluding the new hole I had just made with my hard head.

For no extra charge, Morris pointed out a huge crack in the stucco. "It could be structural. I can recommend a good contractor." Pride of home ownership isn't all it's cracked up to be.

Three years ago water started creating artistic stains on the attic walls. They were interesting patterns, but my practical wife said, "We need a new roof."

"Nah. It's just minor. I'll patch it up after I fix the broken gate on the fence."

"What about pruning that tree leaning on the house?"

"I can't. You know I'm afraid of heights."

"And what are you doing about the weeds?"

"I'll get to them when I finish painting the kitchen."

"And how are we going to pay for the ski trip, my new clothes, your golf clubs and the Disneyland trip?"

"By postponing the work on the house."

I was young and innocent then. Now I call experts.

Morris had arrived bright and early last Tuesday with his crew. They knew what they were doing. I could tell because they all had holes in their pants, didn't use gloves for ripping off old tiles and knew about wind direction for accurate spitting and cigarette disposal. Morris reassured me. "We just finished roofing that church right around the corner."

I assumed he meant he was close to God.

"Please be careful not to damage my new grass," I told him. "We're very careful about our clients' landscaping," said Morris. (*I had worked hard recently throwing baby seeds where once ugly weeds had grown. I was looking forward to fixing the fence next, after my success with the lawn*).

I watched as the crew toiled in the hot sun shoveling rotten shingles onto the tarps and plywood on the ground. I was glad I didn't try fixing the roof myself to save money for another ski trip this year.

I left the house for lunch. I returned two hours later.

"We've been waiting for you. I've got good news and bad news," he said. "The bad news is you've got dry rot and we must re-face the entire roof with plywood." I lowered my head. Morris had given me a reasonable estimate, "but if there are any holes, it'll cost extra for plywood to fix them." There goes the ski trip for next year.

"What's the good news?" I asked sullenly.

"None of us fell through the holes."

I called my insurance agent to see if dry rot was covered because of faulty construction by the previous owner. Mr. Hodkins, the insurance investigator, arrived quickly. He looked everything over, took pictures and said, "Sorry. This roof is so old we can't help you now. The specifications were okay in the Dark Ages when it was built." I was disappointed and thought his humor was rude.

He started to leave.

"Get off my new grass, you idiot! You destroyed my grass. I'm covered for this." He offered $25. I ran him off my property.

Morris and his crew left voluntarily a few hours later with all my money. I stood in the front yard gawking proudly at the new roof I had adeptly installed — with a little help, of course. Then, uh, oh. My feet sank slowly into the mud by the water meter. I had proudly fixed a leak there a year ago. I called Rich, the plumber.

"No charge." I was grateful it was just a loose fitting I hadn't tightened. But he pointed to a large hole by the meter. "Are you aware of your mole problem?"

Oh, no! The lawn!

My wife arrived at six o'clock. "How's your day been?"

"Great!" I lied. "Got a lot done."

"I can see. The roof looks good. But did you see that section of fence lying on the ground by the broken gate where the tree branch fell and killed the grass?"

I picked up the paper to look for apartment rentals.

A Sign Post Up Ahead — a Clean Rest Room?

Many of us just returned from summer vacations. We romped in cramped vehicles, avoiding news about crime, taxes and recession and used up lots of gasoline while it's still affordable.

I'm sure on your trip your most important questions were why you took the kids, why maps don't display rest stops with clean rest rooms and how did America's towns and roads get named?

ZZYZZX is the name on a road sign in a canyon between Los Angeles and Las Vegas. This is true. It was named by a caveman who discovered the free-enterprise system. He began chiseling out a new business for himself writing dictionaries for tourists — he apparently started from the end, but never finished.

On a bridge in Oregon is a sign, *Jump Off Joe Creek*. I stopped in the town nearby. I learned that Joe, the community's founder and owner of the tavern, had introduced bungie jumping in 1880. Unfortunately he was a little drunk when demonstrating a new technique at the wedding ceremony with his sixth wife. He forgot to tie the knot — to his feet!

The town of Nothing, Arizona, has maintained its true spirit in spite of years of publicity. I drove through and was glad to see there was no reason to stop except to take a picture of the bony old cowboy on the porch of the general store. He was smiling as he waved, content with the 105 degree heat and the local *clothes optional* ordinance.

Why are so many roads named after eating utensils? Grand Fork, Little Fork, Split Fork, Middle Fork, Witherspoon and Broken Knife come to mind. I once asked an Ohio farmer what he thought.

"Every time a lost city slicker came by," he explained, "I told him to take the second fork in the road and he'd get lost again. My wife got tired of feeding these dumb, stranded strangers, so we named that road out there *East Fork.*" He pointed East with his pitchfork. "It was on the way to Pennsylvania where we hoped they could find other intelligent city folk they could relate to," he laughed. "Some people are really forked up!"

Big, furry animals also are immortalized on road signs. Bear Creek Road, Bear Mountain Road, Bear Canyon Road, Bear Park Avenue and Bear Ridge Route are a few I remember. I've never seen a bear except in a zoo, on a hunter's wall or at a football game, but you can bet I'll never get out of my car in these unfamiliar towns to find out why these places bear the name. I'm more likely to visit towns like Dogwood, Catland and Birdland.

"There's a road sign up ahead . . . the *Twilight Zone,*" began each episode of the TV series. Rod Serling, the genius behind the series, knew there were lessons to be learned from each destination.

I envision future travelers wandering through the country obtaining historical enlightenment, too.

Watergate Ridge will be posted on a street near a hotel in Washington, D.C., where famous people once gathered for a party. Video Alley will describe the street where Rodney King was immortalized by Los Angeles police. Slap Street will be a popular Beverly Hills destination to immortalize Zsa Zsa Gabor's famous act.

McDonald's Highway will stretch across America; golden-colored overpasses will honor the last vestiges of fast-food restaurants when health pills replace good food. Sleepy Hollow will immortalize the grounds of the Ronald Reagan Library, and Alley Oops will designate a mule trail at Grand Canyon where tourists contemplate a living-on-the-edge experience.

There won't be any more Main Streets because, as we all know, the interesting action happens out of sight on the side streets.

79

Streets of Rage East, South, West and North will criss-cross Los Angeles as historical gangland landmarks. And at the corner of Sesame and Jump Streets, Kermit the Frog won't be forgotten for his contributions to society either.

Super Bowl will be the names of towns where crumbling stadiums are landmarks to mighty battles among gladiators who fought for no-cut, million dollar contracts.

On the Road Again, and *King of the Road* are two country songs reminding us of our natural inclination to find adventures away from home. As future travelers sing *"You Take the High Road and I'll Take the Low Road,"* they too will be surprised by some of the new names they'll encounter. And along the way to somewhere else, they'll also find interesting places that are worth stopping for.

Maybe even clean rest rooms.

Parades Prove America Is Alive and Well

Parades are a curious phenomena.

Except for marching rows of ants, swimming schools of fish and flying flocks of geese, most parades bring out the child in us.

I knew the Rose Parade quite well — I grew up in Los Angeles. Now that I live in the Northwest it was up to Darwin, my father-in-law, to show me what a *real* parade is all about.

He took me to the Irrigation Festival Parade held in the small city of Sequim on the Washington Peninsula. It was an event I *had* to experience, he said — one which proves America is alive and well.

The Festival is the longest on-going event in the state, beginning 98 years ago to celebrate the availability of unpolluted water for farm irrigation. People drive for miles to watch the old cars, tractors, logging trucks and assorted clowns clog up the road for hours. We made our way to Main Street, possibly the most familiar place in America.

Bands made music that irritated my ears like hot chili peppers do my stomach. Children didn't know the difference. It didn't really matter. They were fascinated by the loud honks of fire trucks, the sirens of police cars and the opportunity to gum up their faces and hands with cotton candy.

Macho men played chain-saw games, endured tree-climbing contests and demonstrated their essential axe-throwing skills — something I've *always* wanted to be good at.

I was the fish-out-of-water — a city slicker of the first degree. I was getting a powerful dose of rural America. I asked some observers why they enjoyed the event.

"It makes me feel young," said an energetic woman in a wheelchair. "Last year I rolled myself down the road. It reminded me of when I rode in a big Cadillac as a high-school homecoming princess. It makes you feel important."

A grown man was driving a motorized kiddie-car. I asked him if he had a license.

"I'm too drunk to need a license," he said laughing, revealing the flask hidden under his coat.

The horses were magnificent. Pooper Scoopers proudly strutted behind with their wheelbarrows and shovels, trying to maintain some dignity after being rejected as marching band members just because they couldn't play an instrument. Brave souls, these kids!

The mayor, police and fire chiefs, school principals and politicians rode like legends in their own minds in cars and trucks I've seen only in old movies, car shows, other parades and junk yards.

Darwin proudly explained the utility of the trucks, plows and tractors. He told me how pistons and physics worked together to haul and harvest. I was beginning to feel some genuine interest.

I checked when I got home and leaned that the Mule Day Parade near Dunn, North Carolina, draws 50,000 people to watch the Grand Mule strut its stuff after winning the honor for pulling the biggest load. Isn't *that* a kick!

In Mexia, Texas, the Chairade is a long-standing opportunity to demonstrate the uses of chairs. The locals and a furniture manufacturer put them on wheels and anything else they can find, and attract large crowds away from the local pubs.

I learned from a friend in Jonesboro, Georgia, high school home-coming parades are important attractions. "They tie-up traffic when you're trying to get out of town," said a local. "But the local clubs, high school bands and floats brighten the day, and give the politicians an excuse to practice campaign techniques."

I learned from another friend in Arkansas that life is boring. "We just have the usual Fourth of July Parade and rodeo activities; some day maybe we'll organize a Clinton Day Parade if he does any good in Washington and comes home a hero."

For all the exhibitionists we know, there are those who prefer staying in the background. For each parade, there are probably as many people involved in planning as in participating. A parade is the ultimate test of cooperation between the planners and doers. It's a chance to have a good time, feel important and be acknowledged by friends and neighbors.

"Everybody loves a parade," the saying goes. And I'll always be grateful for the unpolluted water in Sequim 98 years ago. And somewhere out there is a mule waiting to spot me in his hindsight for mocking him as the leader of a grand parade.

Thanks, Darwin, for another life lesson. Farewell, Rose Parade. The truly meaningful parades are those in rural towns where people celebrate the spirit of real community.

Capitalism Flying High in Moscow

Capitalism and military down-sizing have created an ironic twist in Russian-American relations.

A recent ad in the newspaper read: "*Fly a MIG-29 at mach 2.5 in Moscow.**" At the bottom by the asterisk it read, "*No, really. Flight packages from $6,000.*"

I called the 800 number.

"Migs, Incorporated. How may I help you?"
Caught by surprise, I asked to speak to a salesperson.
"Is this for real?" I asked. "Yes sir," answered the polite gentleman in clear English.
"What do I get for $6,000?"
"Three days training in an L-39 trainer, food and lodging. You pay the air fare to Moscow."
"Is the pilot Russian or American? I asked. "Russian, but he speaks fluent English."
"Your ad says I can fly a MIG-29 or MIG-31."
"Sure. After your training and for an additional fee."
"How many Americans have done this?"
"That's classified information, but we've been very busy."
"And what about flight insurance?"
"It's a risky business, and . . ."
I hung up, quickly realizing I hadn't asked the important questions. I called the Florida-based company back.
"Do you get vodka and caviar in first class? Are the stewardesses pretty? Do you show in-flight, surround-sound movies like *Top Gun*? Do you get to shoot missiles at Iraq or New Jersey?"
This time *he* hung up. I think he figured I wasn't serious.
Several months ago I wrote, in jest, about the possibility of dream vacations on submarines, tanks, battleships and jets, after the drastic U.S. military cutbacks were announced. My theory was new travel industry jobs would be created, helping to relieve unemployment. And the cost of maintaining expensive military toys, lonely and forgotten in shelters across America, would be reduced.
I had no idea this crazy idea had any merit. Now there's no end in sight.
Just imagine . . .

"Take me to Columbia," says the drug czar pointing a gun at the MIG pilot in Russian airspace. "I don't have enough fuel," answers the pilot. "And I'm scared."

"No problem. Sniff some of this and you'll feel fine. Then stop in Miami. I have friends there who will help us out."

Or: "Well sir, it will cost an extra $3,000 to surface — then we'll be a day late to our destination."

"I don't care what it costs," says the angry man. "Get this sub out of the water. I paid to catch Alaskan sea bass."

An ad in a local newspaper reads: *"Stressed from daily frustrations? Is your anger building up? Rent a tank today!"* The ad describes how, for a mere $8,000, you can blow up simulated desert towns and city office buildings; or if you bring an 8x10 glossy of your favorite enemy, he or she will be enlarged to a life-size version you can shoot with the tank's radar-guided machine gun — ammunition and psychiatric counseling extra.

"Honey, this was such a romantic idea," says the young bride to her creative groom. "Being married by an admiral on a battleship cruise to the Mediterranean was so exciting. But was it necessary to fire those gigantic guns? You know, my father's heart condition."

"I'm sorry, dear. He's okay now. But I'm sure he appreciated my shotgun wedding joke. When he recovers he'll certainly understand that firing the guns was part of the bargain. He'll be glad to know his daughter didn't marry any dummy."

"Ultimate Adventure," reads the ad in a travel magazine. It describes an around-the-world tour in fighters, tanks, nuclear submarines, landing vehicles, attack helicopters and armored personnel carriers. For $150,000 you travel through Bosnia, Haiti, Iraq, Russia, Somalia and East Los Angeles with trained and experienced military guides.

If you survive, there's a Bonus Plan. For $15,000 the U.S. government, in appreciation for your patronage and trust in its military hardware and personnel, offers you the opportunity to ride in Air Force One with the president and receive, absolutely free, a $200 haircut and autographed copies of the federal budget and health plan.

A $6,000 thrill for a 2-hour flight in a MIG-29 in Moscow? What's next?

Let's reciprocate and help our new Russian friends learn even more about adventures in capitalism. Let's put an ad in a Moscow newspaper. *"Experience Business and Democracy. Spend a week with Ross Perot, Bill Gates and Donald Trump. Learn to Make Billions."*

In the fine print — *"Then spend a month in Congress to learn how it's taken away."*

Finding Interest in All the Wrong Places

My wife is looking forward to the free vacation at the Dude Ranch in Montana. Earning it wasn't easy, but I learned three lessons.

I had borrowed money during the credit union's April promotion, asking for far more than was required to qualify for the gift. I didn't want to arouse suspicion about my hidden agenda.

The story goes like this.

The roof was leaking, our yard offered an alternative lifestyle to our neighbors' weeds, two of four gears in the Honda worked occasionally when coasting down hills, our used clothes were rejected by the Salvation Army, the carpets were bleached through to the floor and the sofa had more holes in it than the O.J. case. I've observed that none of this is unusual in America. That's why credit cards and Dr. Kevorkian are popular.

My wife appreciates my financial philosophy: never borrow money or use credit cards if you have to pay interest — try friends and family first. If that fails, do without. If desperate, get a job. But the free vacation promotion attracted my attention. After discussing the interesting sprouts growing in the damp attic, we finally decided to get into debt like everyone else.

"I'll take care of it," I said, performing the *take-charge-kinda-guy* routine women go crazy for. "There's a special deal at the credit union. We'll get a free vacation."

"Oh, honey. You're so smart and wonderful." (*I believe women use better lines than men, when it comes to getting lucky).*

Chris, the credit union loan officer, was very cordial. She asked the usual, stupid question that no one ever answers truthfully.

"What's the money for?"

"A new roof, landscaping, furniture, clothes, a brain transplant for my editor who lost his mind, car repairs, carpets and psychiatric care."

"Psychiatric care?"

"Borrowing money makes me crazy. You know, the stress. I'll probably need to get a real job." I kept a straight face. Chris smiled politely, glancing at the tax returns.

"Seems like everything's in order. You should qualify."

"Good. When do we get the money."

"Well, we need an appraisal, and the title has to be checked."

"Okay. When do we get the money?"

"We have to check your credit, verify your wife's employment, audit credit card balances and ensure you have homeowner's insurance with flood, earthquake, draught, wind, rain, fire, tornado, sun and bomb protection."

"Fine. When do we get the money?"

"After approval, we need time to get the loan docs prepared."

"When do we get the money?"

"Three to four weeks."

Five weeks later, the loan was approved.

We dined out to celebrate. "Oh honey," said my wife. "I'll be so happy when we get these things taken care of. I know you hate to borrow money. But I promise, I'll never ask for anything again." My wife is a saint. We left McDonald's and returned home.

Three more weeks passed by. Chris called us in.

"Sign here, sign there, sign here, sign there," I munched candies while looking out the window at the beautiful day.

"How much longer? I have a golf lesson."

I picked up the check three days later and deposited it. Then I *immediately* wrote a check back to the credit union, paying off the loan without interest. Clever, clever — I gloated silently to myself as I stopped by to thank a surprised Chris for the free Montana vacation. Then I left for three days of golf and fishing previously planned with some buddies at the local lake. I returned home, excited to share my latest act of financial wizardry.

I was stunned. The house had a new roof, there was a new carpet, a new used car, the yard was beautifully landscaped and my wife looked great in her new clothes.

"Surprise! See, I can get things done too! After the loan was approved I used the credit cards to have everything finished before you got home. And we won't have to pay interest on the cards because now we have the cash from the loan to pay them off."

I sank heavily into the new sofa.

As I said earlier, my wife is looking forward to the Dude Ranch vacation. She's taking her son. I can't go. I have to find a job.

But I did learn three good lessons. 1) Pay lots of interest to important needs; 2) Pay *more* interest to your spouse; 3) If not interested in Lessons 1 or 2 — and you want to be a *take-charge* kinda person — credit cards will help.

Real Fortunes Found in Hard Work, Not Cookies

"Great fortune will soon match your talent," read the inscription in the fortune cookie.

"Money comes from surprise source," read the newspaper horoscope for the day.

I didn't work last week. Instead, I waited patiently for these prophecies to materialize. I watched with increasing excitement the goodies advertised on the *Shopping Channel*, deciding how I was going to spend the big bucks coming my way.

87

ADVENTURES IN THE SLOW LANE

Then at another Chinese restaurant I read the fortune cookie message with confusion; *"Don't spend money foolishly. A rainy day is coming soon."*

In Washington State, that's not much help. It rains a lot. Then I read today's horoscope. *"Female family member needs attention after emotional outburst. Volatile Scorpio is your ally."*

There aren't any Scorpios in my family. I'm the only one who has emotional outbursts. And I'm still waiting for free money. I began questioning the value of horoscopes and fortune cookies.

There is great historical significance in fortune telling. Just ask any economist, political pollster, weatherperson or sports bookie how they reach their conclusions and you'll recognize how you, too, can be a fortune teller. "I study the facts, based on scientific research," they say, "and then make my predictions."

Sure.

It's embarrassing for educated people to admit they rely on fortune cookies and astrology. Only Nancy Reagan had the courage to admit she needed occasional guidance from her personal astrologer when Ronald was dozing under the stars.

Let's get real. Have you ever read a *bad* fortune cookie or astrological forecast?

The truth hurts. I know nothing about astrology or fortune telling. But I can make predictions as well as anyone, even if they're never right. So can you.

In tough times, there might be some entrepreneur out there willing to capitalize on a new concept — fortune cookies containing the *truth*! Here are some examples which might give the tasty morsels some crusty credibility.

"Get a wig. Avoid bad hair days."
"Your mother-in-law is right. Divorce now."
"Love is coming your way. Unfortunately, you're somewhere else."

"If you had intelligence, you wouldn't be reading this fortune cookie."

"Breath spray is your best investment."

"Indigestion and hunger will soon be apparent."

"Beauty is skin deep. Call a plastic surgeon."

"If you eat this cookie, the truth will come out in the end."

"Invest in your future. Buy a rocking chair."

"Diets don't work. This restaurant appreciates your patronage anyway."

"Laziness causes anxiety. Enjoy your depression."

"All good things must end. Avoid disappointment. Take a break and procrastinate."

"There's light at the end of the tunnel. Unfortunately, it's an oncoming train and you don't have a return ticket."

"Keep this fortune. It's the only kind you'll ever have."

"Don't air your dirty laundry. Words are easier to clean."

"Riches are floating down the river, but you're on a bridge. Jump now if you believe your fortune."

Predicting the future is frustrating. Every time I read a fortune cookie I hope therein lies the truth. But I'm still wondering why my talent hasn't brought that great fortune and where the surprise money is coming from.

I was inspired, however, by the kid across the street.

"My daddy said the harder he works, the luckier he gets."

That made sense.

I decided to do something about it. I wrote my own fortunes.

"Computer-games byte off creative thinking. Go back to playing with words."

"If you want to be a writer, write something."

"One person's humor is another person's anger. Write with much care."

"Glamour doesn't pay bills. Get a job."

89

It was difficult to write anything important this week because I was lazy — until I found this awful, but truly inspiring fortune in a cookie just hours before deadline.

"If you don't work, you don't eat."

I paid for the lousy meal with my last $5.

At least the fortune cookie wasn't stale.

Pay Now or Pay Later: Doctors, Mechanics Get It Anyway

Mechanics and doctors are alike. They make you wait, promise to fix your problem and charge an arm and a leg — and then you get to return to have the same problem fixed again.

A couple days ago the mechanic at the Honda dealer couldn't figure out why there was water in the trunk. I went to a parts store later to replace a brake light. The clerk replaced it and a gallon of water gushed out of the plastic enclosure! So much for expertise.

I once complained to my doctor of chest pains. He told me to stop playing basketball with the kids. I described the pain to my barber the next day and he told me to get checked for heart problems. Two days later I had a heart attack! Go figure.

Okay, nobody's perfect. We expect doctors and mechanics to be God-like. But I'm tired of paying lots of money, spending lots of time and constantly being irritated. I figure *my time* is worth something, so I'm considering deducting $50 an hour from *their* bills for the time I spend waiting in *their* offices for *their* services!

This morning I overheard this conversation at the Mukilteo Coffee Company where all the important townspeople gather.

Mechanic: "We just increased our hourly rate to $47. People will pay anything to save their cars."

Doctor: "You're right. Same for their bodies, although some I see are probably worth more at a junk yard!"

Mechanic: "How much are you getting an hour?"

Doctor: "I haven't figured it out, but it's somewhere around $300. The malpractice insurance is still killing me, and my accountant needs more for his new Mercedes. Golf balls are going up, too."

Mechanic: "I understand. I had to buy an expensive diagnostic device to check pollution emissions and have to pay now for removing oil from the premises. Those environmentalists! I make a killing now on oil changes and clogged exhaust pipe surgeries."

Doctor: "Yeah, I can relate. The other day I had a patient complaining of a sore left foot. I could've prescribed soaking it in hot water and a firm taping, but that was too simple. So I gave him some pain killers, had some X-rays taken and told him to modify his diet."

Mechanic: "His diet?"

Doctor: "I made him believe less weight on his foot would keep the pain from coming back."

Mechanic: "Oh, yeah. That's like the lady who complained her car wasn't starting properly during the winter. I sold her a battery, distributor wires, flushed out the radiator and added anti-freeze."

Doctor: "What was *really* wrong?"

Mechanic: "She only had the problem on Sunday mornings after her 17-year-old son had used the car for a date. He didn't gas up because he didn't want to pump in the cold!"

Doctor: "What do you do when customers complain?"

Mechanic: "Just the usual. I listen with compassion, fix the problem and give them another bill. If there are lots of problems, I buy the car from them, fix it myself and sell it to my friend, a used-car dealer, who sells it for a large profit we split."

Doctor: "That's a good idea. If one of my patients dies, I could offer to buy the used organs and sell them for profit. Or if their body is in real bad shape I could make a deal with one of those fitness and diet clinics for referrals. I send them a bad body, they return it in good shape, and then I could make a killing doing TV commercials!"

ADVENTURES IN THE SLOW LANE

Mechanic: "Ya know doc, we're really in the same business. We'll always do well. Cars and bodies are the same. They both run well if properly maintained, but nobody comes to see us until a problem arises, usually from neglect. Oil changes and long drives for cars, and good diets and lots of exercise for bodies, would almost put us out of business. I'm glad people are lazy!"

Doctor: "Well, I'm not going to argue with you. I still have some ethics, though. I feel bad for those who can't afford health maintenance or insurance. But I have a wife who won't give up the country club and my kids want to attend private universities. It would be hard to change my lifestyle."

Mechanic: "Yeah, me too. Well, it was nice chatting with you again. By the way, here's the bill. Your car needed a new engine, transmission and paint job. It comes out to $6,500."

Doctor: "Thanks. And here's *my* bill for delivering your baby boy. He needed an extra spanking to get him going, and I had to charge extra for getting rid of the smoke your cigar made in the hospital. I got in a lot of trouble for smoking it!"

Mechanic: "You're kidding? Nine thousand dollars! You're out of your mind."

Doctor: "My car was only three months old, pal!"

Mechanic: "My kid was only three minutes old!"

The two shook hands amicably, agreeing to meet again.
I suspect they paid each other — tax deductions, I bet.

Crime Doesn't Pay What It Used To, But . . .

Laws and the justice system are hitting a lot of foul balls lately when we need home runs.

Serious crimes like murder, rape, theft, corruption and taxes rise unchecked, while more laws are passed infringing upon individual rights like smoking, littering, parking drunk without a seat-belt and income-tax cheating.

I have a plan — the New American Dream. It will include a Clean Cop and Arrogant Attorney for *each* American household. This will help increase domestic new-car sales and spur the high-tech communication industry. Custom-made, two-person Law Cruisers, will be equipped with a computer in the back seat for the meticulous attorney to review and interpret laws, and video equipment in the front seat for the cop to film crimes, interview witnesses and watch violent entertainment during crime lulls and donut stops.

To streamline trials and due process, there will be a Supreme Judge in every town with more than 1,000 citizens, law-abiding or otherwise. This will reduce crime, the cost of lengthy trials and outrageous legal fees. I interviewed local citizens who thought they could do a good job as Supreme Judge if elected to serve the public. Only Roy Bean IV was willing to speak for the record.

"Mr. Bean, what sentence would you impose upon income-tax cheaters and insurance fraud criminals?"

"What sentence? How about, 'Congratulations, can you show *me* how you do it?' "

"How would you sentence those who break the proposed new laws coming up for the books?"

"Anyone caught talking in a movie theater would be fined $100 and sentenced to five continuous hours watching the *Weather Channel* in silence. Those driving without a spare tire or litter bag would forfeit their licenses for one year and be sentenced to six months of community service fixing flat tires on buses or picking up election campaign pamphlets strewn along the roads.

93

"Parents administering addictive drugs like ice cream, hamburgers, pizza and candy to their children would be restricted to rice and broccoli for six months.

"Children caught throwing trash in a neighbor's yard will clean their rooms daily for one year. Workers stealing pens or pencils from the office will be forced to sell the stolen merchandise on street corners and reimburse their employers with the profits.

"Swearing or spitting in public will result in demonstrating the use of mouthwash in grocery stores. Men leaving toilet seats up at home will clean public toilets for one month. Teenagers who disagree with their teachers' or parents' opinions will lose daily MTV privileges for each offense.

"Any man who wolf-whistles at an attractive lady will be jailed 30 days with a wolf-whistling parrot for a cell-mate. If the lady's ugly, he'll be nominated as Citizen of the Year for his good deed. Any woman smiling seductively at a man will be jailed in a mirrored cell for 30 days. If *I'm* the object of her attention, the case will be plea bargained in my chambers."

"Mr. Bean, are you sure these laws will be enforceable?"

"I don't see a problem. I've got eight boys and four girls who are looking forward to being cops and lawyers when they grow up."

"What about the law restricting couples to two children if they don't make more than $150,000 a year?"

"Fortunately for us, the law wouldn't apply. But I can assure you, I'll severely punish those who turn their extra children over to their friends or relatives to avoid the taxes."

"But I thought you appreciated tax cheating?"

"Oh, yeah. I'll have to think about that a little more."

"And what about those new laws regarding free speech?"

"Not a problem. It won't be free anymore. Any citizen attending City Council meetings to voice an opinion will be required to pay a speaking fee. If they agree fully with their elected officials, they'll get a substantial rebate; if not, they'll be required to pay an enormous surcharge."

"Mr. Bean, you sound like a dictator."

"Nope. Just a law-abiding citizen tired of crime."

"What would you do to serial killers, rapists, burglars, psychopaths and savings and loan executives?"

"Turn them over to Hollywood screenwriters for research — if I get part of the deal, of course — or sentence them to hanging without any chance for parole."

Mr. Bean was locked up early this morning after exercising free speech from atop a picnic bench at the State Park at 2 a.m. But he was so effective entertaining criminals during their prime time, the mayor encouraged him to run for County Sheriff when he gets out.

Crime doesn't pay what it used to. It's more lucrative now.

Just ask any lawyer or movie-maker.

Be Careful What You Wish for

I remember lucky Lucy Lacy's advice in high school to be careful what I wished for because I might get it. I'm not very lucky when it comes to getting what I wish for, but I've gotten a helluva lot more than I probably deserve.

I was shy back then. I secretly revealed to only 17 close friends that I wished to marry Lucy because her father was a rich businessman who owned an airplane, yacht, several fast cars and the local movie theater concession stand.

Lucy had those wonderful personality traits mothers admire. She was kind, intelligent, well-mannered, assertive, self-assured and meticulously dressed. Friends snickered at my questionable instincts for money and influence instead of reasonable compatibility. They also laughed at my belief that Lucy admired me for my intelligence, good looks, athletic prowess and my vivid imagination.

Lucy ended up marrying a man of great strength, integrity and wealth who overlooked her minor exterior deficiencies in favor of good character. Fortunately for me, I discovered, much too late, my friends' judgments were superior to mine. After struggling

95

unsuccessfully for years to find wealth and success on my own, I married a woman endowed with both extraordinary beauty and character whose only flaws were bad judgment in mate selection and insufficient income to feed my waning dream.

I saw Lucy recently at our high-school reunion. She was dazzling, although when she walked away from the bright lights, her diamonds, emeralds and rubies couldn't conceal what aging does to a person — even one with wealth.

"Hi Lucy, you look great! How are you?"

"Knock off the bull. I see you haven't changed much in all these years. What are you up to these days?"

"Well, I finally got lucky and found a good woman who doesn't care how much money I have. She's a real gem."

"Yes, I can appreciate gems. What do you do for a living?"

"Write a newspaper column."

"About what?"

"Stuff."

"I see you're still not sure of yourself."

"Yeah. I'm pretty good at that, Lucy. How are you and Bill doing these days? Still traveling a lot?"

"Not really. Bill and I are divorced. He was caught in the junk-bond scandal — used his profits for the presidential campaign. Spent some useful time in prison, wrote a book and used the money to defray legal fees. I don't speak to him anymore unless I don't get my alimony check."

"That's awful, Lucy. But you're still lucky, aren't you? Bet everything else turned out swell."

"I suppose. I got the house, Mercedes, jewels, custody of the kids and the food processor."

"That's great, Lucy. How are the kids?"

"They all graduated from Harvard Business School. The boys are still in prison. They built a large, successful drug-smuggling business, and our daughter is night manager at McDonald's — some business school!"

"I'm sorry. I guess luck isn't hereditary. Seems like we didn't get what we really wished for after all, did we Lucy?"

"I can't remember what we wished for. It was so long ago."

"Well, I remember wishing to marry you so I could enjoy your family's wealth and have it rub off on me. I think you wished for travel, fame and the good life."

"Yeah. That sounds right. I got it too, didn't I?"

"Well, so did I, in a sense. I hitched around Europe for a year and once got to interview Wilt Chamberlain while he stretched in a limo. I was even famous for a few days after I appeared on TV to explain an editorial I wrote."

"Really?"

"Yeah. I wrote that golf would someday be more popular than sex, food and football."

"Geez, you always *were* a little iffy off the tee," said Lucy.

"Well, maybe just a little. Is that why you weren't seriously interested in me in high school?"

"No. That's why I *was* interested. You were the only one who liked me for who I was, rather than a rich sex object."

I hesitated. "Yeah." (*And my friends had claimed it was I who had the imagination!*).

"Good to see you again," I lied. "I hope you still get everything you wish for."

When I arrived home I hugged my wife, watered the lawn, fed the dogs, made a hamburger and read the paper — and rejoiced that these simple, wonderful activities were not what I had wished for.

Poor Lucy. She still doesn't get it.

Dialing for Dollars — A Confusing Game

Dialing For Dollars was an educational TV game where, if you were the lucky person who sent in a post card and were called by the station, you could win lots of cash by answering important and difficult questions.

"Okay Mrs. Smith. Get this right and win $150 in our lucky jackpot. Who was the man with the big ears and mustache who used the first swear-word in a popular movie? You've got 10 seconds. (*Suspenseful music playing*). Okay Mrs. Smith, what's your answer? Oh, I'm so sorry. No, it was Clark Gable in *Gone With the Wind* who said, 'Frankly, my dear, I don't give a damn.' *Mr. Ed* was a good guess, Mrs. Smith, so you win the souvenir TV schedule for our next 220 movie classics."

It's a different game today. Now, dialing for dollars is a mega-buck industry. Unfortunately, *we* do the dialing but the long-distance telephone companies get the money.

AT&T and Sprint are two names that might ring a bell, but *Ma* won't answer because she's all broken up. The resulting competition keeps long distance calls moderately priced but the promotional advertising is causing great confusion.

"Thank you for calling AT&T. How may I help you?" says the polite operator.

"Yeah. I'm interested in the Reach Out America Plan. I understand I get discounts on all calls."

"Do you make more than $8 worth of calls a month?"

"I'm not sure. I can't differentiate between the calls and the taxes. But I want to save money so I can make more calls."

"We offer 25 percent off night and evening calls between 11 p.m. and 8 a.m., 10 percent between 8 a.m. and 5 p.m. and 30 percent between 5 p.m. and 11 p.m. How does that ring your bell?"

"I don't know. If I call too early or too late, I wake up my mother. I can't stay up late enough or get up early enough to take

98

advantage of the other time period, and day calls cost too much even with the discount. Why can't you just give the same discount for any time? This gets too confusing."

"I don't know, sir, I just answer the phones."

"Well instead of all the discounts, why don't you just lower the costs altogether?"

"That's too simple. We have to compete with the others."

"Yeah, I guess. I thought of getting that discount service with the other company to get free calls to friends and family that I call often, but then I realized most of them don't want to talk to me anyway. Then I figured, if I talk longer, it's costing more than I save on the discount."

"I can understand your concern, sir. You might consider logging all your calls for six months, evaluating them based on time of day, length, distance, weather conditions, subjects of your conversations and number of people spoken to at one time. You might even try our 10 percent discount on conference calls. You can call up to six people at once and share the gossip saving postage, and . . ."

"Thanks. I'll think about it."

"Good afternoon. Thank you for calling Sprint. We appreciate your business. How may I help you?"

"Yeah, I just talked to AT&T. They tell me I should log all my calls for six months to determine which savings plan to enroll in. I'm so confused. Do you have any suggestions?"

"Sure. Try each company for six months and see which bill is lowest. Then stick with that company until it changes its plan. Then compare again."

"Not a bad idea. But it will cost me more to make the switches than the calls are worth. May I ask which company you subscribe to?"

"Oh, sir, I can't give out that information. The Privacy Act, you know."

"You're right. I'm sorry. By the way, how much is this call costing me and your company?"

"Oh, it's free, sir. No charge to either party. We offer this 800 number as a good-will service to provide you the opportunity to discover how well you can hear us."

"Oh? I heard AT&T is offering a new, high-tech hearing system that makes it sound like you're sitting right next to someone — no extra charge."

"That's true, sir. But you can hear me very well now without that service, can't you?"

"Yeah, you do sound pretty good. Are you married?"

"Sir, the Privacy Act."

"Sorry."

No matter which long-distance service you have, you save money using the adage, "*The more you talk, the less you're heard.*"

I can't play *Dialing For Dollars* anymore. It's too difficult without an advanced accounting degree.

Escape: It's Better Than the Alternative

Recent escape stories in the media have released some interesting thoughts from the prison in my mind.

The escapees have cheered me up considerably with their successes, however temporary, and reinforced my belief that imagination can run wild more freely than reality.

A very large cat escaped from the zoo and ran wild in Philadelphia, obviously misinterpreting the true meaning of the Liberty Bell. Five murderers in Florida received answers to their prayers while burrowing their way to freedom under their prison church known for its encouraging and inspiring sermons.

A successful robber escaped but foolishly turned herself in for a reward she wasn't eligible to collect. Instead, she was rewarded with the annual *Stupid Person Lives Here* sign on her jail cell. And

Newt Gingrich escaped for months in spite of his book deal, until his mother made her own with Connie Chung for the *whisper heard 'round the world.*

After discussing these events with local deadbeats, I visited the prison where another friend is getting early retirement benefits, including three squares a day. He avoided the IRS for 37 years using a phony Social Security number but got caught when he accidentally used the real thing applying for retirement. He's always been a good source of wisdom about worldly things.

These events, says my friend, represent what any *real* American believes: "It's better to escape, than the alternative."

Here are more seriously flawed historical anecdotes that validate my friend's profound axiom.

In grammar school I eluded Mrs.Thatcher's evil stare while throwing spit wads at Mary Lou. In college I was finally caught and expelled for tossing a Vodka-filled orange to Bonnie in an advanced horticulture class.

I escaped my mother's wrath by falsely accusing my kid brother of eating all the ice cream, but was nailed later when he showed her my college Zoology project in the back of the refrigerator. (*I later made a change purse out of the dissected rat's skin for my mother, but she still didn't care much for the poor fellow*).

As a budding teenager, I once evaded work by putting my entire weekly paper route product into a dumpster. I got away with it because there were no grocery-store coupons that week, so nobody complained. However, I got caught and fired the next time because I didn't know about the personal ad in the classifieds: "*Reward for information leading to the arrest and conviction of the newspaper bandit.*" I'm not sure who turned me in, but I'll bet it was my brother who was bigger now and still angry about the ice cream incident.

I avoided the Draft during the Viet Nam era, claiming myself exempt and incompetent as a college student, but begrudgingly got bagged into a uniform when my attendance records and intelligence tests revealed consistencies with my claim.

ADVENTURES IN THE SLOW LANE

I avoided a major embarrassment when my best college buddy reinforced a big lie. He confirmed to my new girl friend, who was wealthy, beautiful, wonderful, but not too bright, that I had graduated with a Ph.D. in Astrology and had signed a contract with NASA as an astronaut. At the wedding ceremony shortly thereafter, however, I was caught for my lie. Three unemployed buddies from the local bar showed up drunk just moments before the minister spoke the bondage words. One shouted out: "Hey pal, now *you* can afford to buy the drinks every night." I lost my prized catch.

I once eluded four survey-takers at the mall by disguising myself as one of them. I even had the appropriate pen-on-a-string attached to my clipboard-with-a-form. I was exposed when asking a very attractive woman if she would mind spending a few hours filling out the 18-page cookie questionnaire at my place. I told her we could then determine if Mrs. Butterfield's Cookies were as tasty as my home-made goods. She had a loud voice. "Security!" I escaped.

I remember once escaping out the back door of an expensive restaurant after I accidentally set the place on fire fumbling to light the candle on the table. I returned a month later to the remodeled eatery. This time, an alert waitress watched me turn the fake candle upside down trying to light it. It didn't help my cause that I was wearing asbestos gloves. This time I was caught.

To escape writing something intelligent and complicated when I wasn't up to the task, I once wrote a column I thought was ridiculous and silly. It was about how to build a personal atomic shotgun. I was accused of misleading the public by an anonymous reader. In a letter to the editor he described how I miscalculated the amount of plutonium needed to power the deadly weapon. As far as I know, he hasn't been caught yet.

It's better to escape, than the alternative.

Imaginative escapism is surely more liberating than reality!

No White Elephants in White House Garage

Our annual, city-wide garage sale was very successful.

I was too, managing to seize a bag of reclaimed, battered golf balls (*some were suspiciously familiar*), three landscape plants and a real find — an antique garden hose found in the Sahara Desert.

Spending little for valuable items is stimulating and satisfying. But allowing others to scavenge through your personal possessions is awkward. It's humiliating to admit you even *own* certain items in your household. It's like selling vintage mayonnaise, mustard and catsup that have been aging in the frig for a year or two. I'd feel guilty taking more than five bucks a bottle.

Garage sales are interesting because you can watch ordinary people become sophisticated hucksters. Some displayed $5 necklaces on velvet pillows. Used clothes were neatly hung from metal racks with signs reading: *"One day sale. Fifty percent off all marked items."* Unmarked items must have been worthless.

One lady was selling canned sodas from a dispenser. You could buy one for 60 cents or the whole machine for $800. One-day liquor licenses aren't legal, but the mayor, who owns a micro-brewery in the basement of his pizza parlor, was selling political favors by offering "half-off" cold ones in exchange for warm votes.

A woman selling an oil painting of a famous president told me, "It belonged to my great, great, great grandmother. It has great sentimental value. It's a steal at $75."

I'm not a thief, nor a fool. I offered $10. "No deal."

Imagine a White House garage sale. People hanging out there really know how to sell to the American people. *"One Day Only. Everything must go. Fifty percent off. Help reduce the deficit. Save your country. Own a piece of history."*

Some of the items for sale:

Item: Eighteen-minute blank Nixon audio tapes with one-minute message. "I'm not a crook. I had nothing to do with

Watergate. Here is what I have to say about the subject . . ." $38. With expletives, $99.

    Item: Antique vacuum cleaners from the Hoover administration. $19 each.

    Item: President Kennedy's love letters from Jackie, $1. From others, $575.

    Item: Billy Beer from the Carter administration, 49 cents/six pack.

    Item: LBJ's Great Society inspirational postcards from the San Diego Zoo, $1 each.

    Item: Bill Clinton's roach clip, used when he didn't inhale, $12,000.

    Item: Hair treatments used by Presidents Eisenhower and Reagan. $99/ bottle.

    Item: Saddam Hussein's autographed self-portrait given to George Bush for Christmas. Includes 18' x 36' frame, $19,000.

    Item: Hillary Clinton's health-care plan, 39 cents. With shipping crate and postage, $400.39.

    Item: Nancy Reagan's stale fortune cookie collection, $1,300.

    Item: Oliver North's international, mail-order weapons catalog, $120 million.

    Item: Federal vacation guides to Haiti, Nicaragua, Somalia, Kuwait, Detroit, $1.

    Item: Sets of original sheets for Lincoln's bed, $500 each, while they last.

    Item: Autographed copies of Jimmy Carter's *Playboy Magazine* interview, $150.

    Item: Vintage Reagan jelly beans, $3 each. With special caffeine formula, $15 each.

    Item: Lady Bird Johnson's original rattlesnake chili recipe, 5 cents a copy.

    Item: LBJ cabinet meeting tapes, uncut with expletives, $15.99. Translated copies for non-Texans, $29.95.

    Item: Jimmy Carter baseball peanuts, $199.95. Oval Office Peanuts, $299.

Item: Original bullet from Ronald Reagan assassination attempt, $3 million. Replicas, $5.

Item: Matching pairs of left-foot Gerald Ford walking shoes, $199.

Item: Newt Gingrich balanced budget proposal, $1. With scale, $24.89.

Item: Bill Clinton's original draft notice, $1. Copies of deferment notice, $400.

The way I figure it, a White House garage sale is a good way to get rid of government waste. There's enough room there for more white elephants than just presidents. And there are plenty of fools who'll spend anything to own a piece of history.

I thought I was immune to this insanity until I learned the oil painting I didn't buy from that sentimental woman was an original of Andrew Jackson. She found out it's worth $375 thousand and donated it to the Smithsonian for tax deductions.

At my garage sale this week, I couldn't sell my classic Underwood typewriter or the manuscript of my first column. Since I'm no dummy, I donated them to a collector for tax purposes, too.

The garbage collector only charged me $5 to take them away.

Football Widows No More

Analyzing the male psyche and its need for bathroom reading, fishing, boxing and football, is always an interesting topic among confused women and deranged psychologists.

These pastimes, no doubt, give men a sense of well-being but, unfortunately, lend credence to our reputation for arrogance. Let's take football, for example.

The Season has started and so, once again, many women are relegated to Football Widows — a somewhat sexist label, since I know at least two women who prefer *watching* a game to serving their husbands and cleaning up after them.

Men generally hate being restrained from being men. The first rule, ladies, is never *hold* your husband against his will during play; in football language, over zealousness in a *prevent* defense can result in a 10-yard penalty and possible loss of down. (*In extreme cases, loss of husband!*)

You know the old adage, "If you can't lick 'em, flatter 'em." *The Season* is an opportune time to learn to maintain wedded bliss.

Learn the game, ladies; it's the flattering thing to do. He could be overjoyed to share his expertise (*ego*) with you. And, believe it or not, you might teach him a thing or two! This shared experience might go like this:

SHE: "Honey, why did that tight end drop the ball? Should he be drinking before the game? Maybe they should use Velcro on the ball and their gloves."

HE: "Very funny. What? You're serious?"

SHE: "Sure. The guy who throws the ball could sew Velcro on his backside and stick the ball there when he pretends to give it to one of those guys who run funny. Then he could run the other way and nobody would chase him."

HE: "Right."

SHE: "Why is that guy dancing like that, honey?"

HE: "Didn't you see that great catch? He scored a touchdown."

SHE: "I'm sorry, dear. I was finishing the *TV Guide* crossword puzzle. Is that good?"

HE: "Why do you think he's dancing?"

SHE: "I don't know. Why?"

HE: "Um, because he . . . don't ask stupid questions."

SHE: "Sorry. It's very confusing. First he dances happily; then he throws the ball down like he's mad."

HE: "Yes, dear, it's confusing."

SHE: "Why don't the referees wear something more fashionable than striped shirts? Baseball umpires look so sophisticated in their tuxedoes. These guys look funny."

HE: "I don't know."

SHE: "Oh my God! That huge guy almost took that little guy's head off. Why do they have to be so brutal?"

HE: "Because it's their nature. It's called intimidation. Next time that runner won't go his way."

SHE: "He'll just go run somewhere else then, won't he? What's the point?"

HE: "Never mind. It's too complicated to explain."

SHE: "How come they always wave at the camera and say 'hi Mom' instead of 'hi Dad?'"

HE: "They're just showing off to their moms."

SHE: "Kinda like when you almost broke your back trying to impress me by moving the refrigerator yourself without my help?"

HE: "Would you please get me another beer? Wait! Wow! Look at that! A draw play on fourth down! What a call! They made it! First and goal."

SHE: "What's a draw play? Is that something those guys on the sideline do on their note pads?"

HE: "No, honey. The quarterback lets the defensive players almost get him, and then at the last second gives it to the runner. If there's a hole in the line, the runner can sneak through for a gain."

SHE: "That's a great play. I understand, I understand!"

HE: "You do? Great!"

SHE: "It's the same when you chase me into the kitchen when I'm not in the mood. I let you get close, then at the last second I hold up a beer. You stop. I hand it off to one of the kids who runs outside with it. Then you chase him and I get back to my reading."

HE: "Yes, dear, that's exactly right. Football teaches deception, grace, love and happiness. Now I know why I like it better watching games with the *guys*!"

SHE: "Why, dear?"

HE: "Because. We don't have to explain why we're men. And that's why we *never* go shopping with you."

SHE: "Oh?"

HE: "In football, the competition is measurable. There are interesting statistics, violence, excitement and an end we can bet on. When you shop, the score is always more than we can afford."

SHE: "What are you doing this afternoon?"

HE: "There's a half-price sale on fishing gear at Big Arnie's today. I've gotta get there quick before the good stuff's gone! Do you want to go with me?"

SHE: "No, honey. I think I'll go over to Sheila's. We're all going to watch the afternoon game and decide who the best-looking and most informative commentators are."

So much for attempting marital bliss during *The Season*.

Well, we tried!

There's Money in Keeping Secrets

I've got a secret that could save us all lots of money.

My information was validated by a story written by Jeffrey Smith of the *Washington Post*, which said that 32,397 hard-working, lip-locked people are employed keeping our nation's secrets secret. The total cost is estimated at $16 billion annually, but the actual figure is protected by several highly-paid, trusted government workers whose identities are guarded by a few mysterious others whose salaries are also closely shrouded secrets.

Supposedly, federal documents are classified to protect us from obscure security risks like, perhaps, Eskimos seeking winter homes in, say, Laredo or Palm Springs.

There were more than 6.1 million bits of information classified in 1993, according to an audit by the Office of

Management and Budget, the article said. This might include the information that White House toilets were flushed 26,124,438 times last year, indicating, at 5 times per day per person, that there probably were 1,476 people per day living in, visiting or maintaining our president's house, and they ate and drank a lot.

This is important information because if conquering enemy real estate agents wanted to sell the place as a theme park after an invasion, they would have to know how much to charge for admission and where to place the waiting-line ropes and refreshment stands.

Obviously we need to continue spending taxpayer money to protect national secrets. The CIA, Department of Defense and National Security Administration no doubt have long-term contracts with weapons manufacturers and shredder-machine companies. In order to save vast sums of money, however, they might use the White House sewage system instead of shredders. But the loss of secret jobs would add to the real unemployment figures which are secret because poverty is a touchy subject with our bureaucrats. Oh, well.

Who determines what documents are to be classified? That's secret, of course. But, by using clandestine journalism techniques, I was able to find an amateur Deep Throat at the White House McDonald's, the newest, chic insider hangout President Clinton has made famous. My source used napkins to scribble notes for a book she's going to write in prison to put her kids through college, after she's caught and arrested.

Here are some of her revelations. These facts are classified, so please keep them secret, otherwise *you* could be arrested.

The White House chef told a friend that President Clinton hates broccoli and loves jelly beans, but doesn't want anyone to know he has anything in common with Republicans. Hillary bought heavily into McDonald's stock before taking office.

Secretary of State Warren Christopher was excited about getting his name in the *Guinness Book of World Records* when he ate an entire Big Mac in one bite after removing his foot from his mouth.

A Pentagon official said we are considering an invasion of Haiti because the present military leadership there won't allow us to build a Congressional golf and tennis retreat until we legalize drug imports. He also said we've stayed out of Bosnia because his colleagues can't figure out how to tell the good guys from the bad guys and they haven't been able to lock in any movie rights for a military invasion because nobody in Hollywood gives a hoot.

A Gillette and a Remington company executive each gave his lobbyist a huge bonus for convincing President Clinton to support the Israeli-PLO peace agreement. Apparently Mr. Arafat has agreed in principle to a shaving commercial, to assure his followers that smooth faces will guarantee future political concessions and provide employment opportunities in barber shop franchising.

A record company executive was overheard telling a CIA operative that the copyright to the Beatle lyrics, *"Listen, do you want to know a secret, do you promise not to tell, oh, oh, oh,"* will be released to all politicians for campaigning in exchange for leaks of secret information, once they're elected. And I'm sure everyone already knows we're about to file bankruptcy and exile our entire teenage population to Singapore for appropriate punishment.

There are no secrets in this world, folks. I can find out anything I want in *The National Enquirer* or from neighbors.

Let's save $16 billion by eliminating government secrets.

Life Is the Biggest Game Show of All

Game shows are popular. You can live vicariously through others' good fortunes and momentarily escape from boredom.

I was having a bad week, so I immersed myself in a fantasy of game show mania. It was quite an experience. When the price wasn't right, I made a deal to spin the wheel of fortune and found myself in jeopardy. When I didn't win a thing, I became a star on *Peoria Squares*. I watched 26 hours of game shows, including repeats. I yearned for *Beat the Clock* and the *$64,000 Question*, shows you might remember. Today, they would be; *Beat Your Wife,* and the *$1 Million Question.*

As I sat exhausted counting all the money and prizes I could've won, I wondered what the ancient Egyptians might think of the *$25,000 Pyramid.* What an insult to history! I began to ponder about some new shows . . .

Bet Your Life — Three death-row convicts are introduced with rap music as they walk, chained at the ankles, onto the stage. They are greeted by emcee Mike Tyson. They are given their choice of fighting him in a small cage; swimming for three minutes in the alligator-infested Everglades or piranha-laden Amazon; going to Iraq on a secret mission to assassinate Saddam Hussein; or spending the night with Roseanne. If they survive their chosen ordeal, they are spared. If not — enjoy the taped highlights on the next show!

To Tell a Lie — Bill and Hillary host. Contestants are given campaign speeches written for politicians from Abe Lincoln to Jerry Brown. The contestants then make the speeches in front of a video camera. Excerpts are played on the program, (*edited delicately by Hillary*) and winners are decided by studio audience reactions to whether the promises made were actually kept.

The Good Health Show — Academy award winner Anthony Hopkins, our favorite psychotic Hannibal the Cannibal from the movie *Silence of the Lambs,* cooks up his favorite healthy recipes. Contestants must guess the secret ingredients of his concoctions. Winners get free psychological consultations; losers become organ donors for the next show.

Name That Talk Show — Contestants must match talk shows with special subjects and guests. Hosted by Johnny Carson, the show would include answers such as Geraldo, Sally Raphael, Oprah Winfrey, Howard Stern, Montel Williams, Phil Donahue, David Letterman and Jay Leno, among others. Topics would include: Lesbian Bikers and Their Choices of Motorcycles, Tattooed Men Who Date Tattooed Ladies, Daughters of Bashed Celebrities, Victims of *The National Enquirer,* Women Who Love Cats Too Much, Misanthropic Psychologists Who Hate Themselves, Co-dependent Dogs of Abusive Masters, Wanna-be Talk Show Hosts, Game Show Addicts, Disabled Veterans of Political Campaigns, and Abused Victims of IRS Audits.

Name That Pet — Hostess Betty White introduces pet lovers and their pets. Contestants must match the owners with their beloveds, based on the tricks and make-up of the animals. The owners tell why they own pets; the pets perform and the game begins. Snake, cockroach and flea owners must provide their own security.

Make My Day — Hosted by Clint Eastwood, this show offers mystery and intrigue. Mafia soldiers make offers the contestants can't refuse. If the contestant *can* refuse, he or she wins a free trip to New York or Chicago, accompanied by Eastwood, and the Mafia soldier is shot with the most powerful handgun in the world. If the contestant *can't* refuse, the offer is carried out and the results are graphically shown on the next show.

———————

If anyone in Hollywood steals any of these ideas, they will get free psychological counseling. It became apparent to me, after conceiving these ideas, there is a thin line between reality and fantasy. Winning a game show, after paying taxes on the goodies, results in minimal rewards and lots of unwanted, solicitous phone calls — and perhaps a family feud over who gets what.

Life is the biggest game show of all. It has its own rewards and disappointments, too.

Surviving another day is a significant win in itself.

Local Elections Clarify Ignorance and Democracy

Local elections provide deeper insight into human behavior than most interactions except Day-After-Thanksgiving shopping.

Democracy and ignorance are clearly defined when gentle neighbors become savage adversaries on controversial issues.

But something *really* interesting is happening here. Citizens are voting on a proposal to change the form of government from a mayor-council (MC) system to a council-manager (CM) system.

From personal interviews, I've discovered there isn't much difference between the two — either way, politicians will make me pay taxes for things I didn't know I needed or know I don't want.

The MC system is similar to the national president and Congress format where things get done in a timely and efficient manner, because everyone gets along so well and we have someone to blame when things go wrong and someone to joke about. At the local level you can scream up-close and personal because small town mayors usually have real jobs where you can find them.

In the CM system, I've learned, seven Council members can dream up interesting ideas like building mosquito traps for swamps, or prison camps for runaway parents trying to avoid pubescent youngsters. They can mandate their collective wishes onto their hired professional city manager, without the approval of an elected mayor.

One of the Council members becomes a figure-head mayor, handling the important ceremonial duties like attending senior-citizen parties for retired former mayors.

It's like the former Soviet Union where Gorbie and other intellectual leaders spouted off about issues when the Politburo told them to or, failing that, found themselves quickly exiled to lake-front properties in Siberia or otherwise dispatched.

Since it's difficult for a less-than-political non-persona like me to decide which form of government is better, I asked other random, lost voters what they thought.

Lost Voter 1: "I'm voting for the council-manager government because my sister said she saw the mayor take a bribe from Mr. Mozzarella."

"What was it?"

Lost Voter 1: "A hundred pounds of cheese for the mayor's pizza parlor so Mr. Mozzarella's driver wouldn't get a ticket for parking his delivery truck on the railroad tracks."

"Oh."

Lost Voter 2: "I'm voting for the council-manager government because I counted 332 campaign posters for the proposition and only 48 against. Besides, my brother is a friend of one Council member who said the mayor never agrees with him."

"About what?"

Lost Voter 2: "I don't know. Does it matter?"

Lost Voter 3: "I'm for keeping the mayor-council government. How would you know what seven people think? I can get an indirect answer from a mayor easier than I can from a committee!"

Lost Voter 4: "I'll vote to keep the mayor system because I want to run for office when I graduate from high school so I don't have to get a real job. I want to make a lot of money and get the power and influence to change the course of history. I know I can do that here if I'm elected."

"Why?"

Lost Voter 4: "I read the recent best-sellers by Ross Perot, Rush Limbaugh and Howard Stern. This town is *so* confused!"

Lost Voter 5: "I'm not voting. I read all those weird comments in the 'Letters to the Editor' section of the local paper and got so confused by all the gibberish, I decided to let others decide for me. What's the big deal, anyway? No one ever listens to me."

Intelligent Voter 1: "I'm for the mayor system because you need a singular vision for the future in a growing city, and you need someone with the ability and popularity to build a consensus of agreement with that vision. A manager, by definition, manages details and isn't necessarily a leader."

"That sounds pretty good. Who are you?"

Intelligent Voter 1: "Someone who'd like to keep his job. I'm the mayor."

I don't feel lost anymore, now that I've learned so much about politics and persuasion.

Now, if only I could convince my wife about . . .

The Worst Boss Is Hard To Find

A man who prevented his employees from assisting a heart attack victim during work hours, withheld information about a missing employee's death for three days and motivated his employees to work harder with cash advances for booze and drugs, was recently honored in a contest for the worst boss in America.

His business, no doubt, is extremely profitable. He's efficient and expects the same high standards of productivity from his dedicated employees, even those who selected him as one of the 700 contest nominees. He probably gave his nominating committee a bonus for acknowledging his expert management techniques.

Unlike most people, it's been my experience to serve many wonderful and compassionate bosses. (*Too many, according to my wife*). They only fired me for incompetence, absenteeism and stupidity, but never for offering a cigarette to that heart attack survivor, nor for bringing my bookie to a merit review, nor for wearing a red shirt and purple tie at a formal company dinner party. One gracious boss even gave me an extra week's vacation so I would miss his daughter's wedding.

But there were others.

Jim fired me on the spot at his dime store when I was fifteen. A little kid stole a squirt gun and got away. Trying desperately to hold on to my only source of income, I tried to explain why I ran after the criminal with another squirt gun. Jim had no concept of fair play, so on the way out the door I lifted some candy and a $20 camera.

115

Chuck kept harassing me to get rid of my classic 1974 BMW and buy an economy car like all the other employees had. He said it caused him and the company great embarrassment to have the BMW seen in the employee parking lot. I refused to sell it, so Chuck gave my privileged parking space to another employee. When I complained that the four-block walk to the office was unreasonable, he assigned me to the demo car-washing detail.

I left the job at Toyota the next day.

"You are hereby notified you no longer qualify for the company Thanksgiving turkey." The memo, on official company letterhead, was signed by my supervisor, Cliff. I was miffed. Only two days earlier he had said my work was exemplary and I could expect a raise when the company rebounded from its current economic downturn. But being a stickler for company policy, he reminded me that after three tardies, I had lost my free coffee privilege, after six, I had relinquished my 5 percent meal discount, and now, after nine, the turkey.

When I challenged him on how he kept track of my being one or two minutes late once in awhile, he screamed back; "The company didn't give me *this* just to keep my own time," holding up his wrist with the Rolex he got for 30 years on the job. When I objected to the company's petty policies, he fired me on the spot, pointing to the watch, "You've got 2 minutes, 15 seconds to get out of here."

I'll never work at that donut chain again!

Oliver wasn't a bad boss when he was out of town. But when he clenched his fist and threatened me with, "I'll give you an opportunity to use our dental plan," I suspected our relationship wasn't going too well. He accused me of taking a confidential memo about my impending termination off his secretary's desk and then lying to him about it. Of course I had read it, but I pointed to the stack of resumes on her desk, obvious clues about the future of my job. I asked him if he knew much about wrongful termination and discrimination. Infuriated, he called the secretary into his office. Then, red-faced, he abruptly left for the airport.

Fortunately his boss, a wiser man, took me to lunch and offered me a promotion while we reviewed what I knew about Oliver. When I revealed that the secretary had asked for my help in converting expense accounts for golf excursions into business trips, Oliver's boss smiled. When I told him she had joined Oliver on several occasions, he smiled even more. I had validated what he had suspected all along. When Oliver returned, he and the secretary were fired and had to leave all their golf balls behind.

I survived another year, but then got caught taking my new secretary on a golf excursion. I was fired, but got to keep the balls.

The worst boss is as hard to find as the best boss.

I'd prefer none, but what would I do without a wife?

No Justice for Pest Control

"Ouch! I got stung on the toe by a yellow jacket!

I stepped on the ornery critter while it was napping on the service porch. *Rule 1*: Always wear leather boots in laundry rooms.

Ants, cockroaches, bees, spiders, snakes, rats, mice, mosquitos and fleas can be — like insurance salesmen, bill collectors and in-laws, extremely irritating, and in some cases, dangerous.

The bees deployed quickly. The nest was outside above the back door. With two caps, gloves, goggles, two jackets and a can of Death Spray, I approached cautiously. With intensity and determination, I sprayed the nest, watching with delight as some of the enemies dropped instantly and others flew off in panic.

Revenge was mine!

Surprise.

Rule 2: Never spray a pest in a nest — it's best to let it rest.

In the morning I noticed several of my distinguished adversaries swarming in an area directly outside the kitchen window.

I ventured outside. They were scurrying into cracks under the roof. No problem. I got into Bee-Buster gear and sprayed again.

Rule 3: Never believe you're superior to an insect.

No luck. They were still there the next morning — in greater numbers! Some were crawling into the house! Invasion! Professional help was needed.

Wayne appeared at the door. "Hi, I'm from Economy Pest Control. Where are the critters?"

He looked about 60 — scrawny, with tattoos on his arms and I didn't care to know where else. His pick-up truck was emblazoned with *Bug Off,* and he smiled at me with a scary, missing-tooth grin. "I'm licensed to kill," he said. "I'm ready."

He put on his gear. Wearing a netted head covering and white overalls, he carried two canisters of Yellow-Jacket Annihilator Juice into the attic to get the nest, but returned 15 minutes later covered with dust, looking disgusted. "They're between the walls," he said. "I'll get 'em."

When he finished Death Dusting them away, he came in to collect his fee.

"That'll be $106, including tax." I was buzzed away by the price. "What? That's ridiculous for only 30 minutes work."

This Terminator was cool. "Would you want a job like this?"

It was a fair price, indeed.

We talked. I asked him why it's okay to kill yellow jackets, mice and rats, spiders, fleas and ants, but most people resent the killing of porpoises, deer, whales and spotted owls. "Thumper and Bambi created myths," he said. "Mickey and Mighty Mouse made money because they were cute. Flipper and Bugs Bunny made good TV shows, too. And birds that call out in the night saying 'whooo' sound too much like humans."

He showed me his arms. "I love animals," he said, as I looked at the creative impressions of a bat, panther, eagle and dragon. "At home I have three dogs and three cats, a tarantula, scorpion, python, three frogs and a couple lizards."

Wayne was a contradiction. How could a man who loved animals go out everyday killing nature's creatures? Don't they have a right to live too?

"Yellow jackets are mean," he said. "They do no good except pollinating and they're vicious, attacking people for no reason. I won't kill honey bees. They're friendly, make honey and only attack when provoked. I kill only when pests are invading people's homes or destroying their gardens."

Wayne left. I started thinking about the similarity of his philosophy to mankind's thinking when it comes to war and ethnic cleansing. Hitler thought of Jews as pests. The Kurds and Shiite Muslims are pests to Saddam. In America, too many people think of African-Americans, Hispanics, Asians and others as pests invading a Caucasian society. I can imagine how the Native Americans feel.

In some of our small, thriving communities, *anyone* moving into the neighborhood is a pest, disturbing the natural environment and threatening limited natural resources.

When neighborhood kids are throwing trash into the yard and generally making unwanted noise, I admit to thinking about hiring someone to "take 'em home," to maintain some form of tranquillity and protect my sense of security.

It's a paradox that we stress preservation of beautiful natural resources like trees and rivers and porpoises, while simultaneously we destroy so many animals considered ugly and intrusive. We, unfortunately, seem to treat other humans similarly, when we are all really just different animals.

Human pest control will provoke more "stings" to be inflicted by ostracized people. Let's consider assimilating in a more humane fashion before some *real* terminators, perhaps wearing yellow jackets to cover their own ugliness, decide to Death Dust us away too.

A Good Clip Joint

Harry runs a profitable clip joint.

I'm always looking for more lucrative career opportunities, so I made an appointment.

I got a good haircut and an education. In return, he got some good trimmings for use as fertilizer and mole killer in his garden. (*I* knew *there was a good use for previously-owned hair*).

Harry has been running his barber shop only a few years, so I couldn't find ancient copies of *Look* or *Sports Illustrated*. But he did let me scan a book on the history of his business, *Tonsorial Art*. After learning the hair-raising fact that barbers once practiced surgery and dentistry without licenses, and the red on the spiral barber poles symbolized blood from drained customers, I considered myself lucky I've only been clipped so far. But I'll never ask for a razor cut again.

"So how did you become a barber?"

He described his year in barber college. He remembered mangling a practice cut on a mannequin. His instructor drop-kicked the plastic head onto the floor. Harry told the instructor he had created a Charles Barkley Doll because Ken wasn't a good role model anymore. Undaunted by his instructor's lack of humor, Harry continued on the arduous journey. He learned about scissors, clippers, razors, mirrors, brooms, brushes, swivel chairs, shampoos — and most important of all, tact.

"My job is to make people look and feel good. I have to listen to exaggerated golf and fish stories and respond in awe. It also helps if you can laugh at bad jokes. A young woman with long blond hair once asked me to make her look like Dolly Parton."

"What did you do?"

"I laughed like usual and recommended a plastic surgeon. After she stormed out, I realized it's much easier to style hair than build fashionable egos."

"How come you didn't laugh when I said I wanted to look like Robert Redford or Paul Newman?"

"Because you were serious. I didn't want to hurt your feelings. You might write something unfavorable about me."

Good call, Harry.

"So why do other places charge more for a haircut than you?" I asked.

"Mostly ambiance. I don't have to advertise and don't have lots of space or magazine subscriptions to pay for. You know, *overhead*," he said smiling.

"Then you wouldn't give Bill Clinton a $200 haircut? You'd feel too guilty?"

"Sure I'd do it. Eleven bucks for the cut and $189 for my political and economic advice."

"How could you do that?" I asked.

"I know stuff that could be useful in the next election. Politics as usual, you know. Customers tell me how they feel about everything that's going on in town. They complain about the mayor and the City Council, taxes, schools, crime, the high cost of pizza, Little League politics, traffic congestion, sewage disposal . . ."

Just then, the mayor came in. He owns the pizza parlor next door. "Hey, Byron." Harry smiled. "How are you? I'll be done in a minute. Heard you're getting that traffic signal installed. Heard good comments about the Council's new tax plan. Heard your 49-cent, non-fat pizza is a big hit. Heard the police nabbed that O.J. Simpson impersonator at the shoe store. Did Becky find a good plastic surgeon? I'm sorry I offended her. Didn't know she was your cousin."

Harry sure has to know more than just the barber shop business. I was learning quickly this might not be my career choice after all. I can't even sing.

But Harry can. "Sure. I'd like to perform with a quartet at fund raisers," he said. "I'd like to learn more about politics. I might want to try my hand at it someday if I get arthritis."

"From what I saw, you're well qualified already. You were pretty smooth with the mayor, Harry. What tact. And by the way, this haircut stinks. I look more like Bruce Willis than Redford."

He tactfully suggested that I should go for something more suitable to my personality.

"The teens call it a Bowl, a Ledge, a Mushroom or a Muffin," he said. "If you have any English in your blood, I'll do the Muffin for free." We laughed.

No matter how you cut it, a good clip joint is hard to find. Harry warned me that a town barber must be talented, diplomatic and sharp to succeed in this age of cutting-edge technology.

I was disappointed I wasn't qualified for this lucrative career change. Harry understood and let me take my fertilizer home for free.

PART THREE:
Life Is Politics; I'm No Politician

Applications for President Now Being Accepted

Until I applied for the position, I didn't understand what makes a person qualified to be president.

It must be simple because so many others are applying for the job. So I thought!

Mom had once told me, "You can be president if you work hard, do well in school, clean behind your ears, be sensitive to the needs of others, listen well, eat your vegetables ...." The list of obstacles went on and on.

But Mother couldn't have known the successful completion of a 50-page government application form would be a requirement to enter the 1996 race. Here are some of the questions and answers compiled by the Department of Applications and Qualifications, populated with ex-presidential advisers who avoided jail.

QUESTIONS:

1) Which of the following crimes have you committed?
a) Adultery; b) Shady investment deals; c) Failure to pay Social Security taxes on your children's meager allowance; d) Napping during church sermons, political rallies or confrontations with your spouse; e) Inhaling; f) All of the above.

2) You are applying for this position because you: a) Want your kid in a safe, private school where good grades and limousine rides are assured; b) Need a bigger house to entertain your friends; c) Want free travel with triple bonus miles; d) Are good at peaceful negotiations with violent, irrational neighbors; e) Have no job skills and want to get off welfare for a higher-paying government job.

3) The law requires personal financial disclosure. Indicate the value of the following; a) Gun collection; b) Residence;

125

c) Spouse; d) Coin, sports card, hub cap or comic book collections;
e) Stocks, cash, diamonds, piggy bank and stolen property;
f) Dirty laundry.

4) Which party would you join if you didn't enjoy the one you are in now? a) Democratic; b) Republican; c) Independent;
d) Communist; e) Mardi Gras.

5) Have you ever been associated with any of the following clubs? a) Ping; b) Bridge; c) Ornithological; d) Astronomical. e) Anatomical.

6) If elected, to which charity will you donate your tax-deductible, politically-correct contributions a) Washington Monument Maintenance Fund; b) Viet Nam Memorial; c) Watergate Memorial; d) O.J. Simpson Blood Bank; e) Iran-Contra Trust Fund.

7) Which of these important historical quotes best reflects your presidential philosophy? a) "Read my lips"; b) "I'm not a crook"; c) "Don't worry, be happy"; d) "It's time for a change";
e) "Make my day."

8) If elected, which TV show will you most likely criticize?
a) *Star Trek*; b) *Murphy Brown;* c) *Rush Limbaugh*; d) *Sesame Street;* e) *Phil Donahue.*

9) Which personal activity best suits your image?
a) Jogging; b) Yachting; c) Hunting/fishing; d) Horseback riding;
e) Reading.

10) Which world leader do you most respect? a) Franklin Roosevelt; b) Thomas Jefferson; c) Saddam Hussein; d) Sylvester Stallone; e) George Foreman.

ANSWERS:

1) *f.* A good president must be interesting and entertaining.

2) *d.* All answers are close, but most important is the ability to deal with Congress, dictators and the media.

3) Your most valuable assets should be *c* or *f.* Your spouse can be either a great asset or a detriment to your success. Your dirty laundry, if aired properly, will distinguish you historically from most of your predecessors.

4) *e.* It's more fun and appropriate playing a clown in New Orleans than in Washington, D.C.

5) *All*, except *a*. It's important to showcase intellectual superiority if you can't play golf.

6) *a*. An honest, intelligent president is more concerned with pigeon droppings at a tourist attraction than giving more publicity to government fiascoes.

7) *Trick question. All* are correct. Every president says something important and memorable.

8) *d*. Selective irrationality is critical. Criticizing a show that makes pigs, frogs and cookie monsters heroes for our children rather than attacking adult programming that makes aliens, women and talk-show hosts subjects of controversy, clearly shows intuitive, compassionate leadership.

9) *e*. Instead of exposing heavy thighs, showing off your wealth, falling off a horse or killing innocent animals, you've chosen to protect your intellectual image. Of course, your staff will carefully hide your favorites from visitors — *Miss Piggy Goes to Washington*; *Zen and the Art of Roller Coaster Maintenance*; *Wind: How to Make It, How to Break It.*

10) *e*. This obvious winner shows you have confidence in your sense of humor and ability to grow older and wider with dignity. You also know how to attract large fees for future speeches and commercial endorsements.

If you answered all 10 questions correctly, you could become the next president. Based on a composite of the correct answers, a good president should be an honest criminal who cares deeply for his children's welfare, sleeps through times of crises, comfortably wears several costumes at different parties, watches lots of TV to study the social culture of America, has memorable quotes prepared to provide us with important historical anecdotes and participates in interesting and entertaining activities providing job security for writers and stand-up comics who are always desperate for good material.

I didn't get any answers right. I hope I haven't disappointed Mom. She was just trying to give me incentive to get a real job when I grew up. Maybe some day I will; if I learn to fill out an application!

The Rich Don't Always Get Richer — Just Smarter

I had just finished a fine Italian dinner in Seattle.

As I walked out the restaurant door on that misty night, I was greeted by a panhandler dressed stylishly in a brown tweed suit burnished by wear, but obviously expensive when new. "Sir," he said graciously, "can you spare $20 for me and my friends?"

"Twenty dollars?" I looked down the darkened alley where he aimed his nod and saw several men under a tarp playing cards, laughing, smoking and drinking. "Well," I said, "you certainly get to the point. What's wrong with 50 cents or a dollar?"

"Nothing, sir. But collecting small coins doesn't do much for our collective well-being, as you might understand in this economy. Perhaps you'd like to join us for a cup of espresso?"

"What's your scam?" I asked cautiously.

He laughed. "Listen. My name is Geoffrey Salinger. I need $20. If I don't get it from you, I'm going to have to work all night. I don't do windows, nor do I work for minimum wage."

This character was either crazy or brilliant.

"You don't sound like most street people."

"I'm not," he said flatly. "I'm a businessman who refuses to pay taxes."

"Oh, I see. You take money from the rich and give it to your poor friends. You're Robin Hood. See ya, pal!"

"Wait! Look at this. You can deduct the $20." I glanced at the plastic-enclosed card. *Reagan-Bush Era Revival Committee*, it read. It was an official charity tax i.d. card.

"Believe me, it's a worthy cause; you'll be helping us all."

I went along with the gag. "Okay, but first you must tell me who you *really* are."

"I'm a businessman who once owned an aircraft maintenance company. Employed 60 people; then lost a couple government military contracts. Then we were ordered to pay back taxes on profits for the past 15 years because we charged $145 an hour to tighten landing-gear bolts. Soon we had to close down. So here I am."

"Collecting welfare, are you?"

"Yep. So are my friends. But no complaints. We enjoy the tax-free lifestyle."

"You said you were a businessman now. What business?"

"I buy wine and cigarettes in bulk and sell to my friends on the street at affordable prices. I'm worried though about this new sin tax — could put my sources beyond my reach."

"What are those guys playing?" I asked. "Oh, it's the weekly bridge championship. Raymond usually wins though. He was a master until he lost his medical practice. He's our doc out here. Had to close down after they capped his income at $500,000 with the new national medical program. Couldn't keep up with the malpractice insurance and paying those union wages to his assistants.

"Same for poor old Wolfgang. He's the guy over there with the beret and yellow pants. His gourmet restaurant went under when his business customers couldn't deduct lunches or dinners as entertainment expenses."

"How do you guys get by on welfare?"

"It's not difficult. Bill, he's the guy over there with the leather jacket; pools our money and makes investments. He was an excellent junk bond dealer who unfortunately got caught up in the big scandal. Not his fault, I can assure you. And William, the guy with the brown hat, makes sure everything is on the up and up."

"What?"

"Oh, he was a VP at National Bank. His career went south after he made a few questionable deals in the real estate downturn. He's doing community service for six years and handles our accounting. He managed to keep a condo on his way down in the golden parachute."

"And who's that guy in the jeans?"

"That's Leroy our mechanic. Owned a Toyota dealership. Got in a heap of trouble when he declined to pay tariffs on the new pick-ups he imported. He keeps our limo in tip-top shape."

"Limo?"

"Parked at the hotel. We drive VIPs to the airport. Paul, our tailor, made this tweed suit for me." Geoffrey pointed to the smartly-dressed man with the cigar. "He keeps our uniforms in good condition. We take turns driving."

"What and where do you guys eat, and where do you sleep?"

"Wolfgang still has friends at regular restaurants. He barters recipes for left-overs. We eat very well and sleep right here. We take turns using William's condo when we get lucky."

"It seems you all still have your talents intact. Couldn't you go back to real life?"

"Wouldn't want to, friend. The camaraderie is wonderful, we're independent, and we don't pay taxes. Gotta go now. Have to get up early for a meeting."

"You have meetings?"

"Yes sir, breakfast on my friend Senator Burch's yacht to discuss additional funding for the homeless. I hope this drizzle stops."

I gave Geoffrey $20. The education was worth it.

Military Farce Is Fun If You're Not a Soldier

The use of military force in Haiti has reinforced the notion that force *must* support U.S. government policy. Since Uncle Sam seems to be losing some of his sense since he's gotten older, several states are now using their own policies regarding military involvement. The rules of engagement are six months or longer — no shotgun marriages allowed.

Elite units of the National Guard have secretly been dispatched to South Dakota for border patrol duties. The fidgety governor there summoned help to prevent unemployed Californians from emigrating to the precious lands once roamed by buffalo, Indians and Custer. (*You remember Custer. Without the advantage of an Automobile Club Trip Book, he accidentally created a tourist attraction at Little Bighorn).*

A civil war, South Dakota's governor predicted, would soon develop between the invading coastal hordes looking for cheap grazing land and the patriotic, once-conquering neo-natives.

"We need to protect the rights of our native citizens," he supposedly explained to the Pentagon. "We defeated the Indians and we'll defeat the Californians," he exclaimed. "Don't forget. Wild Bill Hickok and Calamity Jane lived here in Deadwood for a good reason." Of course they did. Gun sales took off after the infamous duo exhibited its famous skills. It was good business then.

Incidentally, weapons were once big business in California too. But the Pentagon recently cut capital expenses so it could send troops on R&R visits to vacation spots like Somalia and Haiti. CNN coverage has given future tourists the opportunity to get a glimpse of exciting cultural differences — the use of machetes, for example, rather than guns, to eliminate those with opposing views.

California's governor, unsuccessful in his bid to receive federal financial aid to prevent illegal immigrants from soaking the state budget dry, has now requested special units of the National Guard to suppress civil unrest among all the local immigrants; smokers, gays, O.J. Simpson jurors and used-up guests from Hollywood talk-shows.

"The new crime bill is supposed to put 100,000 cops on the streets," said the governor. "We need them badly, but so far most of them are going to Ohio, Texas, Oklahoma, Florida, Nebraska and Indiana where they're being used to keep college football crowds under control. This isn't fair to the people of California."

Down south, unrest in Louisiana is stirring up anxiety in the melting pot where Cajun cooking is not quite as hot as local politics. The governor there — where oysters, crayfish, gumbo, catfish and jazz are national treasures — is considering military assistance to preserve the state's unique position of national prominence.

"We hafta keep them arrogant Texans from crossing our border," he allegedly said. "They're gittin us bad press, sayin' the

Alamo was really the birthplace of jazz, an' that barbecue is America's favorite food. It's deplorable."

Further north, Ohio's governor had asked for National Guard units to assist the police in Cleveland, where baseball fans were refusing to *leave* the stadium until the players returned the next day in their quest for the city's first championship in years.

"We needed to protect democracy here," said the governor. "If fans want to stay in the stadium and pay for the utilities, then so be it. I'll be damned if I'll allow any team owner and his bully lawyers to evict tax-paying citizens."

Back east, New York's governor, I'm told, has asked for an entire National Guard division to help his police work with the state's new, innovative three-strikes-and-you're-out law.

It works something like this. Incompetent criminals who are stupid enough to get caught three times, get *out* of jail. They get federally-funded training as police officers, hopefully to have a better chance of being productive citizens on the other side of the law.

"We need the extra help," said the governor. "Most of our police officers have only been arrested twice for corruption and aren't yet eligible for parole and participation in the new program."

And in Florida, the governor is preparing his resignation after his request for military assistance was flatly rejected.

"It's totally irresponsible," he said. "Our national leaders help our neighbors up north but won't give us the support we need to protect our own democratic process. I'm afraid the chaos here is coming to an explosive climax. Football fans from Florida, Florida State and Miami University are each claiming they're Number One. They're considering an all-out war to settle the issue."

If policy isn't sound, military force is military farce.

Just ask any soldier.

Tea Party Won't Solve This Problem

Taxes are once again the topic of exciting and ignorant conversations here in Mukilteo.

Proposition 1 is on the ballot to raise money for the police and fire departments.

It seems our city is on the verge of bankruptcy. The mayor and City Council say we can't afford to pay for police and fire protection unless taxes are raised. They say other city employees are over-worked and need more help, too — but how can anyone be sure?

I suspect some of the money might really be needed to build a secret, underground security shelter for the bureaucrats in case of a citizen uprising protesting their dubious management skills.

We don't drink a lot of tea here, so there's little chance of a historic re-creation of the great party in Boston I missed some years back. But we do drink a lot of espresso, so maybe we could dump some caffeine in Puget Sound. It might stimulate the diminishing salmon population to reproduce faster.

I wish I could vote intelligently, but the only sources of information are the local paper, town meetings and gossip — which, combined, confuse me more.

Most people are too lazy to read about taxes because it's boring — until they have to pay. They're intelligent enough to read the police blotter, grocery store bargains and, when desperate, this column. But they don't show up for town or Council meetings unless celebrities like state legislators make appearances to discuss critical issues. For example; how they saved taxpayers' money from being pissed away by voting *no* on new urinals for the Capitol rest rooms.

It's frightening to think how uninformed most of us are on the critical issues of the day, other than what's playing at the movies and what's for dinner. So we're left with gossip.

As one average, ignorant citizen, I asked other average, ignorant citizens about their views on Prop. 1.

A young carpenter: "Well, the 60 cent per $1,000 tax on the assessed value of your property only costs about $5 a month if you have a $100,000 house. That seems reasonable to provide salaries for 18 more cops and 16 firefighters."

"Where do you live?" I asked.

"I rent an apartment."

An elderly woman: "I'm voting no. My house was reassessed by the county at $749,000. I can't afford more taxes from my fixed Social Security income. Besides, I don't need three more cops and two firefighters. I can still use my shotgun and everything of value I own is locked in a fire-proof safe in my basement."

A middle-aged, balding, slightly inebriated pizza parlor owner: "I won't pay another 40 cents per $100 of assessed value of my house. We don't need five more cops and 12 firemen. What we need is a new City Council. Those people already get paid too much."

"They don't get paid," I said.

"Oh. Well, no wonder they don't work very hard to keep the budget under control."

A 30ish criminal defense lawyer: "I'm definitely voting for Prop 1. It's imperative to preserve our neighborhood security. I plan on building a large home soon, after I become a partner at my firm. The house will have an ocean view and indoor swimming pool. The 16 new police officers and 20 firefighters will provide a more secure future for me. Besides, with all the new crime in town, I'll want the police to keep an eye on my place when I'm busy in court defending the poorly misguided."

Everyone seems confused. I heard from a reliable source that the Council had hired an experienced accountant to audit the city budget to determine if there was waste or fraud. When the Council reviewed his report, his exorbitant fees couldn't be accounted for.

My secret source, a bartender who works at the pub across the street from the pizza parlor owned by the middle-age, balding man, who also is the mayor, said he believes the bond issue will pass because people are afraid of losing the services of the fire and police departments. "You'd never guess how many times I've had drunks and missing husbands hauled away. Which way are you voting?"

"I'm not."

"Why?"

"My brother is a firefighter and my sister is a cop. I'm so confused and angry at the politicians, I'm going to burn down the voting precinct to help them keep their jobs."

Recruiting Violations Diminish International Flavor

I was shocked and angry when I learned about the state-wide policy restricting foreign students from participating in high school varsity sports because of unethical recruiting practices.

Fred, a French student I had recruited to cook gourmet food for us this semester, was told he couldn't join the varsity basketball team. I thought at first it was because haute cuisine wasn't allowed in the locker rooms. Then I learned Fred only likes Coke and hamburgers anyway; not wine and snails.

Fred is grateful he can still play junior varsity — he loves the game—although he *is* concerned about his minimal prospects for success in the cooking class I forced him to enroll in. *C'est la vie!*

This policy exists because some over-anxious prep coaches revealed in their back-to-school essays, *How I Spent My Summer Vacation,* that they had recruited European superstars to America. They should've just written about their summer's academic achievements: learning that Michaelangelo's *David* was the first stoned Heisman Trophy and that the Appian Way was the birthplace of cheer leading, where thousands chanted the original *Kick Butt* cheer, encouraging Roman soldiers to prove their athletic prowess by capturing and bringing home trophies that shine in the light.

The local high school coach continued to explain the recruiting problems while he gave me a free golf lesson.

"At some schools, if a coach doesn't win, he or she is booted out between goal posts with no extra points for competency." Since I still can't play better golf and the coach still has his job, I feel relieved to know *our* schools don't share this "win at all costs" mentality. Unfortunately, it probably also means I couldn't play better even if I could afford professional lessons.

As I missed an easy putt, I wondered if I had also missed an earlier opportunity to have an exciting and profitable career as a Super Recruiter. I began reminiscing.

I could see those innocent faces. Five-, six- and seven-year-olds — dreaming of stardom, after-game goodies and thinking "hit and run" meant it was okay to hit the ball and run off the field to the outhouse. It's the summer of '89 — T-Ball — my first coaching job — pre-season parents' night. Only this time, it's different.

I begin. "Good evening. I know you're concerned about the new eligibility requirements for the elementary school sports program. Here's how it works: If your child can throw the baseball from third to first without any bounces, run from home plate to second base without falling and can count, give or take a few, the number of players on the other team, he will be accepted for the program."

"What about the clothing and book allowance?"

"Yes, the program continues to provide free clothing and educational materials. However, if you want the "Ultra Sags" or the CD-ROM version of *Gambling On Your Future* by Pete Rose, you'll have to pay extra."

"Will our kids be allowed to pass the written exams so they can qualify for graduation to the middle school sports program?"

"Sure. I've made arrangements with several high schools to provide tutoring. If their athletes are on academic probation, they can maintain their eligibility by helping others advance in the program."

"And what about transportation?"

"No problem. If you live within the school district, your child will receive limousine service if he maintains first-team status at any level of the program. If you live more than 10 miles away or your kid doesn't make first team, you get bus service. If he has superstar potential, I'll pay relocation costs to the school of your choice, up to 2,000 miles away, and if he's at the high school level, a rental car will be provided at no extra cost."

"How much will the entire program cost?"

"Nothing. Think of the fifty grand as an investment. When your child makes it all the way to the college level, I'll return your investment with interest. After that, I receive 25 percent of his professional signing bonus and 10 percent of his annual income. I provide the Mercedes."

"What if he doesn't make it?"

"There's always the academic route."

"How does that work?"

"There's a special prep program that has majors in contract negotiating, publicity and media manipulation, sports team investment strategies, athletic shoe endorsements and locker room and concession stand management."

"What if our kid wants to be a doctor, teacher or scientist?"

"See a counselor. I can't make a living recruiting nerds."

"What happens to our investment then?"

"Think of it as a tax deduction."

This American obsession with sports and winning — it makes me want to join the French Foreign Legion. I hear it has no recruiting restrictions and — ah, that food!

I just might qualify. *Viva la difference!*

Cleaning the Spring Cobwebs

Winter has mercifully taken a leave of absence. Hope of spring eternal pervades the country, except in Washington, D.C., where cherry blossoms are the only innocents in an otherwise tarnished outpost of power.

Birds are chirping loudly and often, celebrating the new season and the fine job they did decorating my just-waxed car. It's Saturday. I've intentionally avoided the paper, TV and intelligent friends, to clear the cobwebs from a confused and weary mind.

Cory just left. He's a friend who manages an RV park. He described his grass cutting, picnic bench painting, water pipe fixing, office organizing and plumbing fixture replacing. And, ever so nonchalantly, he talked about finishing the police paperwork on the wife-beating death in one of his trailers. Just another day in the park.

Cory's simplicity was refreshing after an hour spent last week with Clyde, my psychiatrist who relishes prolonged, scrambled discussions on computer technology and Asian history. Talking about "information highways" and the Chinese and Somalian political situations is a cunning way to waste time and increase his income.

As I sit alone, watching the birds snag unfortunate early worms, my acknowledged better half is in the forest taking a simple walk, after listening to my complicated excuses for avoiding mowing the lawn, cleaning the garage, setting mole traps or fixing the roof and foundation of the house. Simple chores, I've always thought, are excuses to avoid thinking. And not to think, I've always thought, is a waste of the only healthy fatty tissues in the body.

But take note, those of you in Washington. *Not to think* may be helpful. Take a break for Mental Spring Cleaning. Do *something!*

For starters, Mr. and Mrs. Clinton, simplify the Whitewater issue. It's confusing us. Admit to everything, even if it's not true. So what if you tried to make a few bucks and helped a friend get a loan and withheld evidence and can't remember doing anything wrong. Tell the American people how you did it, so the less fortunate can learn from your successes and failures.

Find a new Secretary of State who can speak straight to foreign leaders in their own language, not ours. Maybe foreigners could understand our foreign policy better than we do.

Put health-care proposals into easy-to-read chart forms. Then develop a TV commercial that illustrates why "Nine out of 10 doctors recommend Health Care Proposal 8." Let the *doctors* explain, smiling, how we're going to get better care by drastically increasing taxes and decreasing their fees. Let them explain why they spend 12 years in school reading boring books and poking holes in dead people so they can heal the sick and then get sued for malpractice.

Instead of talking about the causes of crime and hiring thousands of new police, let's build a few large prisons in Death Valley, in selected southern bayous or in the Texas panhandle. Put an electric fence around Detroit. Make criminals pay. Don't reward them with comfort and security. Cut out their three squares a day and provide only essentials like bread, water and Twinkies.

Stop playing power games with North Korea. If that country is interested in making nuclear weapons, send them a few of ours — airmail. Tell China we don't give a damn about human rights except those which allow them to buy lots of our products.

Let's get off Hillary's case. She's proved that intelligent and powerful women have a place in society. Give her a VIP pass to the White House kitchen where she can bake cookies occasionally to set an example for those who want to know the recipe for competing with male dominance while maintaining traditional and modern values.

Let gays be happy in the military. Segregate. Get a United Nations resolution requiring each country to do likewise, and let them fight *only* against each other. For the educational problems of the country, make it a crime to disagree with Rush, Jesse, Howard or Phil, Democrats, Republicans or economists or historians. And don't argue with writers. Especially writers who want a simple life watching birds flutter about happily on spring mornings unloading lots of bad stuff onto others.

Best wishes, Mr. President. I hope you can get a few minutes alone in the Rose Garden to clear your mind — but spring isn't all that's in the air. Remember the birds. Take an umbrella!

Balancing the Budget by Robin' It

I ran into Bullhead Bean the other day. I hadn't seen him since he robbed the local bank. It was sad when he got caught because Bullhead is the kind of criminal you'd be proud to take home to Mom. He's extremely generous, gentle, polite, always cleans his plate and has superb table manners — unless he's slumped over after his nine-cocktail, pre-meal ritual. He's up on all current events and can recite Shakespeare flawlessly, excusing his Texas drawl as "better than British, not as bad as Australian."

"Bullhead, how the hell are you? I heard you just got out."

"Actually I was out earlier, but you know, the same old crap," he said, shaking his head slowly. "I got caught borrowing this Cadillac from the car wash where I was working. My friend Al had lost his middle-management job at ITM and couldn't afford to continue leasing his car to look for a new job. Appearances, you know. I was just helping him out a little."

"Weren't you supposed to spend more time in jail?"

"Yeah, but they kicked me out — figured it's cheaper to arrest me again than pay the $25 thousand a year to keep me in."

"What did you do with the loot?"

"Had to pay for my poor grandmother's fourth cataract surgery. She and Medicare didn't see eye-to-eye, so to speak, on the necessity of the operation. We sued to no avail. They lost the paperwork. When they found it two years later, it hadn't been processed because she didn't sign it in the right place."

"Why?"

"She couldn't see."

"Oh. So what are you going to do now?"

"Thinking of going into business with Bob, this clever chap I met in prison. He had a lucrative scam insuring heels on ladies' shoes, lost keys, errant golf balls, broken TV remotes, gopher-hole repairs, bad-hair days and other critical items for active people."

"Was this legal?"

"Sort of. But a retired IRS agent, who got insured for his own IRS audits, couldn't collect on his claim when he was forced to pay back taxes for deducting illegitimate charitable contributions to Michael Jackson's legal aid fund."

"So what happened?"

"He sued Bob and discovered through old cronies that Bob had collected more than $6 million in premiums and paid only $1,500 in taxes. The ex-agent won the case, of course. Bob got five years and a $3 million fine for insurance fraud. The ex-agent was awarded a $25,000-a-year annuity."

"What's the ex-agent doing with his windfall?

"Paying back taxes."

"What kind of business were you thinking about?"

"Let's just say for now we're going to be money 'jugglers,' sort of. With our combined worldly experience and what we learned in the comprehensive prison rehab program, we should do just fine."

"What did you learn?"

"Bob and I won the Senior Achievement Award for our Rich Share with the Poor Program."

"What's that about?"

"We manufactured inexpensive, colorful jock straps. We showed the warden and guards how to make a fortune exporting them to well-to-do Mexican and Chinese farmers and construction workers. You know those countries are booming, don't you? Then we set up a, well, you know, a kinda *laundry-room* bank and an innovative accounting system which provided substantial nest eggs for needy inmates returning to society."

"Geez. Didn't the warden and guards get angry when they found out you were siphoning off their profits?"

"Sure, but who could they report us to?"

"You've got a point. I'm still confused about what you're going to do. Is it legal?"

"Sort of, but I can't tell you exactly. Let's just say we're going to use *all* our skills *and* what we learned publishing our best-selling economics handbook."

141

"I'm confused."

"When Bob gets out, we're going to give back money to the people who earned it and help out those who really need it."

"How?"

"We've been hired to use our Robin Hood trickle-down theory to soak the rich to pay for the poor. What we have in mind, though, may be a little illegal, but it's for a good cause."

"What are you going to do?"

"Slowly embezzle from our new employer and eliminate all those greedy middle men."

"How?"

"By using *all* our skills. We got gigs as economic consultants to the White House Budget Balancing Committee."

Dial 1-900-ELECTME; Receive Free Campaign Poster

Smithers for Senator, Waldorf for Congress, Billings for Judge, Yes on Prop 1, No on Prop 2.

All along America's Main Streets, these and other creative posters are again competing for our attention with the beautiful autumn leaves. TV ads are also unusually poetic again this year: *"In 1993 Billy Joe Robinson voted for higher taxes and didn't pay his. Vote for integrity. Vote for Jim Diddleweiler."*

But colorful leaves are more impressive than these inspired posters and TV ads. It's no wonder voter knowledge is minimal and apathy keeps voter turnout low.

I conducted a local, somewhat accurate poll as part of my new book, *Shock Therapy and Election Reform 2000.* The results indicate only 6 percent of the 10 respondents knew any of the people on the posters and 20 percent of those appearing on TV. Even more shocking was only 15 percent knew what a Democrat or Republican was and only 1 percent could fill in the line, *How does this candidate plan to spend the increased taxes you're going to pay?*

Here's an excerpt from my new book. If I sell plenty of them I'll have enough money for my own presidential campaign in 2000.

CHAPTER 3 — Poster Design Strategies

It's a serious mistake to assume people will remember your name at the polls unless you're Michael Jordan, Babe Ruth, O.J. Simpson or other historically significant contributor to society. As voters drive down their neighborhood streets, you must grab their attention quickly with words they will remember better than the names of their own children and favorite TV talk-show host. Following are examples of candidates who overwhelmingly beat their political opponents using simple and persuasive language.

Vote for Me or Die: This Marine combat veteran campaigned for increasing the police force 300 percent and allowing mail-order gun permits for citizens in crime-infested urban areas. The poster shows him protectively holding a child's hand and carrying four pistols on his belt. Unfortunately, he was shot during an argument with a police officer who didn't like the new policy of commission-only pay for each criminal arrest.

No Taxes, No Spending, No Nonsense: This slogan helped a young accountant win the election in her campaign to charge citizens for public schools, police and fire protection, road usage and other necessities, on an individual, pay-as-you-use basis. She was sued for embezzlement and removed from office for sending her children to a private school paid for with excess sewage-treatment funds.

Stupid People Don't Vote. Smart People Vote for Jimmy: This clever candidate realized nobody likes to hear the truth. Voter turnout broke records and he won by the biggest landslide in his state's history. After two weeks in office, he resigned. While being interviewed by a prominent national newspaper, the former liquor store manager told the reporter he had no idea what he was doing. He admitted he had never voted in his entire life until voting for himself. "It was just a joke." He told the reporter; "I wanted to see if anyone else was as stupid as me. I wasn't disappointed." Jimmy served six days in jail for fraud and was sentenced to two years community service as a political consultant — without pay.

If You Try Me, I'll Try You: This superior court judge in a high-crime city won the election easily. Unfortunately for him, the city had more criminals than law-abiding citizens. He served three consecutive terms based on his campaign promise to release all criminals on bail and probation if they promised not to commit the same crime twice. He was finally murdered by a gang of 237 robbers, rapists and car thieves after he sent one of their cronies to jail for failing to pay two speeding tickets. "Justice," said the city's mayor, "works in mysterious ways."

I'm amazed the posters lining my streets say nothing about the candidates or their positions on the issues. Reading campaign flyers and newspapers to learn about them before voting is a good idea, but too much work.

It's much easier to call 1-900-ELECTME to buy my book. You'll receive a free poster personalized with your picture and some great campaign slogans to shock your neighbors.

Who knows? Perhaps you can be a winning politician too!

Zap Gun Simplifies Ethnic Cleansing

I've struggled for months to write, without offending anyone, about the ugly war in the former Yugoslavia. That's difficult to do.

Congress, our president, NATO, the United Nations and leaders of the warring groups offend everyone — with murder, indecision and the tragic fear of being politically incorrect. We've all struggled, and we're all offended anyway. The arms embargo should be lifted quickly to give the players in Mother Nature's dirty little game equal opportunity to survive, or die with dignity.

I'm not smart enough to know who to root for — I just want the killing to stop. Ethnic cleansing is a lousy excuse for marking territory and eliminating those you don't like or understand.

I wonder. If I had a magical Zap Gun that removed people I didn't like to another place without harming them, would I be a happier person if I "cleansed" my town?

I ran the experiment last week. A pick-up driver swerved in front of me dropping several rocks from his over-loaded truck onto my newly-painted Honda — Zap! Two teenagers shove their way in front of an elderly couple to get the last tickets for the first showing of *Batman Returns* — Zap! The middle-finger salute wasn't good enough for the villain who pulled in front of me for the parking space at the market — Zap!

While walking one evening, I zapped several barking dogs who didn't approve of our little cocker spaniel. And I Zapped a few people who frowned at her when she politely fertilized their yards. And 20 taunting teenagers disappeared after they buzzed me with those silent, dangerous roller blades.

At a City Council meeting two members dared to raise their voices in support of raising taxes — Zap! Two others, apparently aware of my new weapon, were conveniently absent on their own when voting took place on a leash-law measure for city streets.

Zap — the mayor was gone when he tried to forcibly remove me from the podium before I could complete my six-hour speech on freedom of expression. I noticed how often I was using the Zapper.

I eliminated the loud and annoying cries of battle when I Zapped the two five-year-olds next door during their raucous midnight squirt-gun fight. In the early morning, I could smile when the Zap Gun provided an answer to the squawking crows arguing over which would be first to feast in my garden, and I exterminated the trash collector who, for some reason, always rattled my cans at the same early hours while I slept.

145

On a real bad day, I Zapped the waiter who simply forgot to bring catsup with my French fries. The minister who reminded me it was better to forgive than to Zap, got himself Zapped without any remorse. Angry at myself for this indiscretion, I pointed the gun at my own head but quickly forgave myself, so I could Zap the cop who ticketed my dog for jay-walking without a leash.

I began thinking of the people in my past who had gotten in my way. I never got along with Harry, the barber, after he made me look like Bruce Willis — Zap! Then to Bill's Tavern where I Zapped the bullies who wouldn't give me a good seat during *Monday Night Football*. I didn't like the way Mrs. Marple looked at me when I ran through her rose garden — Zap! My neighbor Art, poor fellow, is still looking for his son Russ who refused to eat my stir-fried oysters and gleefully poured them down the sink. It was real fun Zapping all those nasty critics in town who thought my columns were offensive.

Did I have a good week? Do I feel better now that I've Zapped in words those who irritate me? Is it true that the "pen is mightier than the sword," if it relieves anger without inflicting physical pain?

If the arms embargo is lifted, I will send plenty of my magical Zap Guns, along with instructions for local use, to those killing each other. I hope they will conclude, as I have, that if you Zap everyone who bothers you, loneliness and the monotony of sameness would be more intolerable than the insignificant irritants.

If this doesn't work, the struggle in Bosnia and other parts of the world, will continue to offend all of us.

Freedom Going Up in Smoke

It must be interesting working the tobacco fields these days.

"Hey, Joe. Look what I found. An orange leaf with a tag on it. It looks real official."

146

"What's it say, Murph?"

"'Certified Nicotine Free. U.S. Department of Agriculture.' There's some other gibberish with code numbers and stuff."

"It must be that experimental mutant plant we heard about at the employee motivation meeting. Better leave it alone."

"Hell no. I'm taking it home to smoke it. If it doesn't satisfy my cravings, I'm going on one of those talk shows and blow the whistle. It's an easy way to pick up a few bucks."

"But Murph, you'll lose your job."

"Big deal, Joe. We're losing them anyway. And even if we don't, I'm tired of everyone lookin' at me as if I were some jerk because I support my family by picking tobacco."

"What will you do?"

"Move to Wisconsin. My brother-in-law owns a meat-packing plant. They haven't banned cows yet."

"I'm not so sure. The new Surgeon General's Report said meat causes cancer, heart disease, brain tumors, athlete's foot, bad breath and hemorrhoids."

"Then I'll go work for my cousin in Illinois who owns an ice-cream parlor. You get to sit down once in a while."

"You might be in trouble there, too, Murph. I saw on CNN the government is thinking of taxing or banning ice cream because it's addictive too and causes obesity, diarrhea and bad gums."

"Joe, as they say in the good book, 'frankly, my friend, I don't give a damn!' "

"What book is that, Murph?"

"I don't know — just heard it was a good book."

"I'm getting worried about you. We've been best friends for 20 years. You're not making sense lately, Murph."

"Don't need to. Nothing else does lately anyway. Hey, what's this over here? Well, I'll be! A *purple* leaf with a tag on it."

"What's it say?"

"Ha! How do you figure? 'Nicotine rich, Organic Compound 497. If found, do not touch. Call 1-800-TOBACCO for instructions. Department of Agriculture.' "

"Told ya, Joe. We're living in very strange times. Hey, wanna be on *60 Minutes*?"

"Nope. I wanna get outa here. Let's get back to the factory and see if someone knows about these plants."

"I thought you were worried about getting fired?"

"Well Murph, we've gotta tell *someone*. If our company is putting extra nicotine in the cigarettes and telling us they're not, and the government wants to ban smoking because nicotine is addictive, don't you think people should know the truth?"

"Whose business is it anyway, Joe? What about Charlie who's addicted to sex and Martha who's addicted to Bingo and soap operas, and old Henry who's addicted to sleep and Cathy who's addicted to shopping and . . ."

"Okay. So those Californians are addicted to driving and there are lots of people addicted to baseball and those folks in Texas can't do without barbecues and our bosses are addicted to work."

"Addicted to *other* people's work, pal. Anyway, I think we've worn out this subject. Almost everything we eat or do could be classified as addictive. Maybe we should move to Brazil or Costa Rica and pick coffee beans. So far they haven't proved drinking java causes anything more than high blood pressure, anxiety and a craving for exam cramming."

"Murph, do you think they'll ever ban ugly bald people who drink cheap moonshine?"

"Nah, Joe. You have nothin' to worry about. Nobody could ever prove bald or ugly is contagious to pets and children."

"I'm glad to hear that."

"Can you give me a hand with this jug? I think I drank too much. Don't reckon I can carry it back to the barn."

"Joe, you been drinkin' the real stuff out here? You promised you'd only drink that government bonded, non-alcoholic stuff!"

"Sorry, Murph. Forgot to tell ya Molly left me last night. Said it was on account of she read in the paper something about a new law banning marriages to bald tobacco farmers who drink moonshine. She said I'm hazardous to her health."

A Few Good Men—Very Few

The "don't ask, don't tell" policy for gays in the military might work for them — but it didn't work for me when I was a reluctant Army soldier. Every time I was asked, I told. I was taught to tell the truth. But now I'm going to sue for job discrimination.

Sergeant Brundle stood rigid as I walked into the recruiting office the other day. I noticed the posters of Marines in action battling unseen enemies on land, sea, in the air and at crowded Hawaiian pubs. Some were dressed up spiffy, with colorful medals on their chests and shiny swords on their hips. I was impressed.

"Yes, sir," I said boldly. "I'm one of the few, one of the proud and one of a kind."

"I can see that. So why do you want to be a Marine?" he said looking me over curiously.

"Nobody appreciates me as a civilian. I'd like to serve my country and get recognition with stripes and medals. I also want foreign trips, three squares a day and medical care while learning a high-paying trade I can use when I get out."

"Uh, huh. You're unemployed now, are you?"

"Well, yes, kinda. I just don't have a day job. I moonlight as an avant-garde poet."

And what other skills do you have to offer the Marines?"

"Don't ask. Okay. I served in the Army 25 years ago. Got released for good behavior. I won a rifle sharp-shooting medal. I'm good at discipline; I trained three parakeets to chirp the *Battle Hymn of the Republic* in synch. And I'm fairly adept at writing. Maybe I could pen a modern marching song — like *From the Halls of Riley's Pizza Pub to the Shores of Miami Beach* and . . . ."

"How old are you?" he asked.

"Don't ask," I replied.

"Are you healthy and tough enough for the rigors of combat, able to get up at five in the morning and eat rusty nails, slimy snakes, crunchy crickets and creamed chipped-beef, without a fork or plate?"

149

"I won't tell."

He sat down, shaking his head in disbelief. "Well, I admire your courage to come in here, but I don't think you're serious."

"But I am. I really want to be a Marine."

"This isn't an employment agency, sir. We're so lean and mean now each Marine has learned to drive his own tank, fly his own plane, shoot missiles, haul heavy equipment on his back and even cook his own food. You want that?"

"Wow! It sounds like a chance to restore my manhood."

"What did you do with your manhood?"

"Don't ask . . . well, my ex-wife, a naval officer, took it — along with my savings, home, children and my '65 Mustang. I've got to find gainful employment again, something that pays well to help with the child support and something that impresses women so I can get back into circulation. I want to be a leader of men *and* women."

"And why, sir, do you think you can be a leader of men?"

"I coached T-ball and Boys' Club basketball. Carried around a big bullwhip. I got those little brats to do everything right. Even won a couple games.

"Besides, after finishing basic training, I intend to complete high school. Then I'll get a Ph.D. in Political Science, become a General and work in the Pentagon supervising top secret global strategies. Then I can get good retirement benefits, mingle with dignitaries and be interviewed on CNN during outbreaks of war."

"You seem to know what you want, sir," said the stern Sergeant Brundle. "But what top secret global strategies could you possibly supervise?"

"Don't ask, sergeant, and I won't tell. But if you don't sign me up today, I'll have my lawyer talk to your superiors and straighten things out with you."

Baaamm! "See if this straightens things out," Sergeant Brundle said with a punch to my mouth. I wiped my bloody lip as I slowly got up off the floor. I gave him my *killer* stare, prepared to fight back, but couldn't clench my fist — arthritis. He chuckled.

"Call your lawyer. Tell him we need a few good men. Very few. And if he wants to sue me, I'll be glad to give him someone to call at the Pentagon."

"Who's that?"

"Your ex-wife. She's in charge of recruiting."

If I had stayed in the Army, I'd probably be a Colonel by now. Or a private in the brig. Either way, I was never qualified physically or mentally to be a soldier. They never asked back then.

If they *had* asked, I would've told. It would've been better for both of us. They eventually found out anyway.

Two Sides to Everyone

Citizens and journalists who chastise politicians for lack of action and judgment have always intrigued me. Criticism, after all, is an American virtue — it's fun, and we do it often and well.

Since little attention is given to *their* views of *us*, I obtained a recorded a conversation between two members of Congress to hear what *they* think.

This clever accomplishment was consummated at a Washington, D.C. dry cleaners by a lady friend of mine with a micro-recorder under her dress. She got a job there pressing bodies, allegedly with help from a former senator from Oregon.

The conversation has been carefully edited by a friend at *The National Enquirer*. Real names have been withheld pending a secret investigation of my clandestine action by the covert operations wing of the CIA's shrouded Sting Division.

"I'm sick of these letters, Axelrod. My constituents must think I'm God or something. They want more crime prevention, better roads, clean air, free medical care, honest politicians and retirement benefits at forty five. But they don't want to pay for it!"

"Yes Brenda, this public servant stuff is a glob of dung. We take all this abuse for a lousy hundred grand a year. But it wasn't much better when I owned my own business. I made plenty, but got sick of paying taxes. My employees wanted more money and benefits, less hours and better working conditions, and they didn't want to work harder for them. *And* they didn't want me around to supervise."

"Yeah. I guess we're kinda lucky no one watches us."

"What? When was the last time you ran into Sam Donaldson? That idiot makes me sweat. He thinks we know things we don't and asks questions to make us look stupid. The other day he asked if I favored term limits, then smiled and asked if I was retiring this year. And those folks at the *Post*. Pheww!"

"I'll only appear on *Larry King*. He makes me look good."

"I think you *always* look good, Brenda!"

"Careful Axelrod. You're pushing your luck. If someone heard you, there would be a grand jury investigating us for inside trading. Remember, I voted against the Sexual Harassment Act because you helped me out by influencing passage of .the regulation excluding taxes on domestic help for Congressional members."

"Yeah, I see your point. Someone might misunderstand. My kids and brother-in-law really enjoyed working at your house last summer caring for your grandchildren. They didn't pay taxes."

"So how are you enjoying your town meetings, Axelrod?"

"Pain in the butt. I've gotta sit there acting Congressional-like with cramps from lousy food while thinking about my wife's threat to leave me unless I spend more time with the family. Then I have to stuff my pockets with names and numbers of people I can't stand and give them the usual 'I'll get back to you on that' routine."

"I agree, Axelrod. I'm especially weary of those pro-abortion community action groups. Every time I come home they confront me with threats to march in front of my children's homes."

"Are the local police supportive in controlling crowds at all thirteen of their houses?"

"No. The chief is single and single-minded. My hometown has only 10,000 people, and he claims the crowds provide an excellent opportunity to party and meet women."

"Oh."

"Have you started planning your next election campaign?"

"Yes, Brenda. I've hired my sister-in-law part time to help. She's well-connected, has civic experience, knows where my opponent's garbage is hidden and can skillfully unclog the obstructions to my re-election."

"That's great! What does she do?"

"She's a county plumber."

"What about you, Brenda?"

"I'm quitting and going into business."

"Wonderful. Doing what?"

"I'm using the new government subsidies we legislated to fund what I deserve for serving the public. I'm starting a day-care center for my grandchildren. Then I'm buying the local newspaper to make sure corrupt politicians get what *they* deserve!"

"Whoa! I've never heard you talk like that. Are you bitter?"

"You betcha, Axelrod. There's an old saying, 'People who can, do. Those that can't, become politicians.'"

"That's unfair, Brenda."

"Probably. But after 40 years in Congress it's time to see if I *can*. It will be very satisfying using my government pension to try."

———————————

There are always two sides to every story.

"Contract With America":
The Circus Comes to Town

This is my first attempt at being a movie critic.

I've chosen the new political thriller, *Contract With America*, as my first victim.

The story spins wildly around three unemployed clowns seeking to win control of the U.S. government.

Eager to please their former audiences who are now constituents in this new circus, they form three rings in and around the White House. The rings are "party circles." Here the donkeys, elephants and mice eat and drink merrily, plot winning strategies and kick, stomp and scurry to obtain campaign funds. The circles represent Democrats, Republicans and Independents. We're allowed only infrequent peeks into the goings-on within the circles, obviously to build suspense that something's not quite right in America.

The three leading characters grin suspiciously as they lead their respective parties in the high jinks — Slick Willie Burger, Nude Gingwitch and Ross Parody. Each character uses his unique talents to prosper. Slick, impressed with George Foreman's knockout punch, adopts the motto "breakfast of champions" to entice followers to stuff cheeseburgers during morning workouts.

Gingwitch, meanwhile, brews up a political cocktail called *Contract With America*. He's seen praying that everyone will believe clowns can become serious. Ross uses money and parables to persuade his constituents he can "two-step" his way around Washington's grid-locked dance floor.

Unfortunately, this absurd triumvirate propels this political thriller into a blundering comedy of errors. Director Steve Feelburger, known for bringing to life believable characters — an alien with a giant red finger and smart dinosaurs that eat stupid people — has regressed with this latest effort.

Nude quickly exposes his lack of credibility when he appoints a 92-year-old senator to obstruct the AARP's demand to maintain eligibility for Social Security benefits for people over 65 — even if they're dead. He never quits. After discovering Senator Jeppe Helmsman (*a staunch, hard-line conservative*) is a homosexual, Nude, without remorse, persuades the embarrassed senator to redeem himself with the impossible task of undermining the loyalty of the southern military establishment.

Willie is more believable. He develops a serious case of indigestion and motion sickness from bad eating habits and shifting back and forth over issues. He's hospitalized with "Bush's Revenge." To do his bidding while he's ill, he hires an accomplished attorney, his wife, with funds they obtained in a questionable, but profitable investment. She quickly adds $20 billion to the federal deficit with a health-care plan. Incredibly, it becomes law just before tainted hamburger is pumped from Willie's stomach, preserving the last of the couple's savings and devouring ours.

In one scene, with his multitude of followers waiting in the wings, Gingwitch burbles, "Wow, what a great disguise I've created. When I was a clown, the makeup and clothes made people laugh. Now, with a few choice words and a few bucks, I'm making these people believe I'm serious. This is fun."

In the Democratic center ring, Willie whispers quietly to an illegal Haitian immigrant, "Don't worry. After Haiti is rid of the U.S. military, I'll make sure your countrymen will all have high-paying jobs. We'll clean up the place. Then I'll have my Hollywood friends build studios to attract tourism and business."

In a sideshow, Parody is seen in the Circle of Mice roaring at a group of Texas and California well-wishers. "Let me tell you, folks. The next sucking sound you hear will be my new Mexican vacuum-cleaner company collecting billions of pesos. And when we take back America, I'll stick the hose in the other end and create the biggest windfall for economic opportunity since the Great Depression."

Phil Donahue, except for the hair and obstinate personality, is miscast as the conservative Gingwitch. Willie is desperately portrayed by a strained Alan Alda and Ross is played gingerly by Pee Wee

Herman. The soundtrack, a modern rendition of *Send in the Clowns*, is raucously rapped by Hammer.

It was difficult to follow the dialogue during the private screening at home. My wife ate popcorn loudly and bothered me with whispered questions about what was going on. She insisted that a serious film critic should view films in a reality-based situation.

In reality, this film is absurd, without structure and frighteningly true. The transformation of the clowns into power brokers never works, nor is it clear who ultimately survives. I barely did. I had to sit through it for this review.

I refuse to endorse *Contract With America*. I give it two middle fingers up. Let the circus move on.

PART FOUR:
Mirror, Mirror, Off-the-Wall;
Who Am I, Anyway?

Scrooge and The Spirit

Scrooge "bah-humbugged" his way awkwardly through the holiday season to avoid *The Spirit*.

He was a self-reliant and prudent man, not having much time for matters of the heart, but plenty for matters of his business.

He was afraid of ghosts, especially his own — those of his miserable, miserly, meandering, meager and motley past.

I have a theory, however, that good old *Eb* wasn't really so bad. He was just a good fictional character created to define *The Spirit* and what it could do.

Each year at this time, I anticipate with some personal qualms, the showing of the Charles Dicken's classic *A Christmas Carol* on TV. The story makes me think of my own ghostly past and my possible transparent future.

Determining which ghosts are real and which are imaginary is difficult. It doesn't really matter though, as long as *The Spirit* is with you. I collected my thoughts on this subject while sitting against a tree. I closed my eyes and enjoyed the tranquillity, disturbed only by sudden gusts of wind blowing crisp winter leaves across the yard. Remembering these ghostly thoughts wasn't easy, I can assure you.

A little boy was holding something gooey in his fragile hand. He reached out to a little girl offering to share his goodies with her. She didn't like snails, though, and the little boy was hurt. He left and quickly returned with two Christmas cookies. She grabbed them both and ran away with an impish smile. He beamed with joy.

ADVENTURES IN THE SLOW LANE

A clumsy, disheveled teenager with slicked-down hair combed into a ducktail was wiping tears from his face. A beautiful cheerleader strutted away with her nose in the air, refusing his invitation to the high school Christmas dance. Later, at the event, he was enjoying the warm, glowing presence of a less-pretty, but classy young lady, even as he stepped clumsily on her toes like a bear while trying to dance as a graceful swan.

A concerned soldier was lifting the body of a drunken comrade. He carried him to safety just before the MPs arrived outside the bar. I could still hear that painful cry; "Linda, Linda, I love you." It was just before Christmas. He had no money to go home to his family. He was leaving soon for Viet Nam. The soldier pulled $200 out of his wallet. "I got lucky at poker last night," he lied and gave his Christmas savings to the grieving friend.

There was a fleeting scene where I saw a college student discreetly passing a large envelope to a big classmate who played on the football team. Somehow the grateful giant got his term paper turned in just before the holiday break deadline, keeping him eligible for the Stumble Bowl. After the holidays, he brought a gift to class for his pal as a gesture of gratitude, only to learn the ghostwriter had to leave school for lack of enough money to continue.

In another scene, I was feeling very lonely at school in Switzerland. I could almost feel the touch of my friend's hand on my shoulder as he assured me I wouldn't be alone at Christmas. His family welcomed me in their home in Germany. I foolishly allowed the wrong Spirits to get the best of me — and unfortunately, the best of their guest bed. I remembered being suddenly not so welcome.

Then, there was that toothless, broad grin on the little 8-year-old face of one of my basketball players just before a recent Christmas. He sank that free-throw in the last minute of the last game for his first and only point of the season. Also grinning on the sideline with *The Spirit* was the referee who, very carefully, called an unwarranted foul on the opposition to give the kid the opportunity.

But the thoughts that kept returning the most were those of friends with *The Spirit* who twice gave me some of theirs after my two heart surgeries, each just before the holidays.

Humor has been *The Spirit* to which I most owe my survival. Although I had many opportunities to use it for more charitable deeds and didn't, it was good to visit the ghosts of Christmases past as a reminder that even a crabby old writer has some redeeming qualities.

I suppose I've never really been as bad as Scrooge, except with the IRS. That's unfortunate, because I think he was a great and memorable character and not really so bad. That's my theory.

I'd like to be remembered that way too.

If Silence Is Golden Why Am I So Poor?

Silence is golden, let's get rich is an adage I never listened to because I was too busy talking to hear it.

Talking a lot has helped me get off without paying traffic tickets and escape confrontations with bullies who were going to hit me until I explained I couldn't hit them back because I had a bruised finger and low self-esteem. Talking loudly and obnoxiously has also resulted in being excused very early from sophisticated parties. You know, the kind where you wear shoes and beer is served in glasses.

The squeaky wheel gets the grease is the adage I *have* followed, but it's worked better for others than for me. Bill Clinton, Madonna and Rush Limbaugh are good examples. If silence is golden, then how come they're so rich and I'm so poor?

I told my soft-spoken wife I was going to become a *silent majority* for one week — I would be low-key just to see how much richer my life could be. I logged the results to use for background data in case I was interviewed later on important talk shows.

———————

During dinner at a local restaurant: "How is your meal, sir?" asked the waiter.

"Lousy."

"What's wrong?" I could only smile. He left confused, and my wife frowned.

What I would have said before the experiment: "The steak is overdone, the potatoes are mushy, the water's warm and I ordered corn, not spinach, moron!"

Visiting with liberal friends Lars and Marlene: "So, Gary, what do you think about invading Haiti?"

"Oh, well."

"What about the poor starving people in Somalia?"

"Hmmm."

"How about the health care bill?"

"Oh, well."

"What's wrong?" asked Lars. "You usually have something to say about everything. Are we bothering you tonight?"

What I would normally say: "The invasion of Haiti is stupid, unless we use rubber bullets, make a video game of the action and give every soldier a free case of rum. Those people in Somalia are learning about over-population. That health care bill would create more government waste and all that debate and research only kept Hillary from baking cookies. And I think you liberals should worry more about changing your baby's diapers instead of talking about the dirty affairs of everything else wrong with the world.

After seeing *Natural Born Killers:* "What did you think of that?" asked my wife in the theater lobby.

"It was okay. The popcorn was too salty though."

What I was thinking: "All right! Did you see that guy's head blown to bits? Loved that scene where they massacre all those prison guards and laugh on the way out. That was fantastic! I could almost smell the smoke from the guns when they shot that guy in the saloon. Wow! She was so sexy when she slit that guy's throat. It was great!"

In the shopping mall with my wife: "I'll just be a minute. There's a special on shoes here. Why don't you have a cup of coffee?"

"Good idea, dear," I smiled. She returned an hour later.

"Couldn't find anything on special in my size."

I smiled again. "I'm so sorry, dear."

What I wanted to say: "Damn it, what took so long? I could've had lunch and played nine holes of golf. You didn't buy anything? Nothing in your size? Why don't you call first? Why do I have to go with you? Why can't women make up their minds? Who invented shopping anyway?"

To our plumber who maintains our plugged-up toilet and bathtub. "What happened this time?" he asked.

"I'm not sure."

"It looks pretty bad. My best estimate is sixty-five bucks."

"Fine," I said quietly.

What I would normally say: "You dirty, rotten, grease monkey. You fixed it a week ago and said you got all the tree roots. Why should I pay a hundred bucks? You guys are all alike — taking advantage when we're desperate. I told you last time I wasn't paying the bill and I'm telling you again. Fix it right this time, or I'll sue your scummy . . ."

"Okay, okay," he says. "Give me your last bill and I'll give you a credit."

"I can't. I flushed it down the toilet last night."

———

The experiment was a great success. I was rewarded with richer and more relaxed relationships with a waiter, a plumber, my wife and her friends.

Silence may be golden, but it's not as exciting as being a squeaky wheel rolling along the quiet, dusty trails of life.

Don't Bluff Wisdom to the Young

I mistakenly taught Cory and his friend Russ to play poker.

It's probably not a virtuous game to be teaching 11-year-old kids, but it's a worthwhile skill for use in real life where the luck of the draw is just as important as learning to call someone's bluff.

The mistake wasn't explaining that a full house was three cards of one number and two cards of another, and not a birthday party — or that five cards in sequence is a straight, not the opposite of a crooked.

My error was believing I could beat them using superior intelligence, skill, worldly experience and great wisdom.

The 26-cent loss didn't bother me as much as the cracks in my fractured ego. A few days have passed since then, and now I've noticed that the two of them believe in me even less than before.

I explained how the Richter Scale determined the severity of the Los Angeles quake, and they laughed. "We watched CNN, and we could *see* how severe it was."

I couldn't argue, so I asked them if they'd like to learn how Joe Montana throws a football. They raised their eyebrows, grinned and sauntered with an attitude into the yard. It took only three throws to brilliantly illustrate my technique. They were compassionate when we returned from the emergency room.

"Don't feel bad," Cory said. "You haven't practiced as much as Joe, and your old muscles are tired." Russ was more practical. "We'll help you fix the window when your arm gets better."

Humility has never been one of my attributes. It was difficult for me to have children question the value of my vast experience.

I was explaining the merits of negotiating with the school bully after Cory came home with a black eye administered by Ralph.

"When I was your age, our school bully called me a *sissy*. When I agreed with him, he said he was going to punch me and I said okay, but I still wasn't going to punch him back. So when he hit me right in the face, I fell over, screamed and kicked and cried. My friends weren't surprised by my cowardice, but after the bully left and

I got up laughing, they had a lot of respect for my acting abilities. He thought he proved something but I made a better point."

"What was that?"

"It's not worth getting beat up to prove how brave you are. Sometimes it's best to take the shot, and keep your pretty face intact."

"Oh," said Cory. "I get it. I should have tripped Ralph once instead of twice when he ran away. I didn't want to hurt him too badly, but he was so big that when he fell he broke his nose!"

One evening I interrupted the boys as they were playing *Streets of Rage* on the Sega. "Come here, I want you to learn about democracy and freedom."

They sat indignantly on the sofa, arms crossed, as I forced them to watch the evening news. Boris Yeltzin was shown struggling to keep a grip on power in Russia.

"Some day you'll learn how important it is to know how the world works so you can survive. I don't think you'll learn much playing those violent games on a TV screen."

I explained how free-enterprise, patriotism and world leadership combine to make America strong, and why Russia was having such difficulty.

"Mr. Yeltzin kids, is trying to change his country's economic and political system to give people more individual freedoms and a chance to make more money for a better life like we have."

"Cool," said Russ. "Look at all those people standing around waiting to buy food."

"Yeah," said Cory. "I hear you can make lots of money selling bread and Levis and other things for lots more than they're worth and there are these tough, powerful guys around, like in the Sega game, who'll protect you from getting caught."

I tried to prove my wisdom was unquestionably superior to theirs, but learned wisdom is measured not by age, but perceptions.

I did, however, impress them with the bald spot on my head, enlarged veins in my legs, my car, three pair of glasses for different occasions, old photos of me in an Army uniform and interesting patterns of lines running down my face.

"There are some things kids, that you can only obtain with age and experience."

They smiled. "Can we play some more poker?"

"Sure." But I wasn't going to attempt bluffing them again.

Be Careful What You Wish for — It Might Be a Nightmare

I got a check in the mail for $655,000.

It was accompanied by an elegant letter of apology from the Treasury Department for errors in income tax I paid during the past 25 years. I was stunned. This had to be mistake.

I thought about the common fantasy — what would you do if you found a paper bag filled with bundles of hundred dollar bills? Take it to the police for a possible reward, or take your chances?

I chose the latter, hoping the IRS computer had lost its memory and would forget me forever. I deposited the check in an electronic teller machine. My checking account immediately bulged to $655,012. I wondered how long it would take to get caught.

I didn't tell friends about my good fortune. They would try to be protective and turn me in for "my own sake."

I started slow. First, I bought a pair of jeans. I waited a week. No IRS, no bank. Then I bought tires for the car. I waited another week. Then I splurged and bought that surround-sound TV-stereo system with the ultra-remote control that regulates the volume automatically according to noise levels of kids, and tunes out commercials. Still no word from the bank or IRS. I was feeling lucky.

The Las Vegas trip was great. I lost only $8,000, but gained eight pounds and bought some leather pants autographed by Elvis. I was beginning to enjoy my new-found wealth.

Things began to pick up. I told the boss to take the job and "shove it," but he was delighted I was leaving! Oh, well. Next was the purchase of a new car and boat. But the schooner wouldn't fit into the garage, so I bought a new house with a bigger garage and a larger living room for the grand piano I was going to buy and learn to play with all my free time. I moved into the place quickly. It's amazing what cash can do.

A few days later the doorbell rang. It was the cops! It was all over, I thought. Not yet. I was relieved. They gave me a warrant to appear in court to pay overdue parking tickets. I smiled reassuringly, knowing I could now easily afford such petty expenditures.

When I came home after splurging on another new car, I noticed the front door was open. The stereo, TV, boat and one car were gone. So was the new computer and the piano bench. But they didn't get the piano or the gold-plated toilet seat — stupid jerks!

I was frightened, so I sold the new house and moved into a smaller one. I didn't want anyone to know I had anything valuable, so I bought diamonds and put them in the safe deposit box. I sold the new boat and one of the new cars and the gold-plated toaster-oven. I bought some vacant land in the country to grow wine grapes, then flew to Switzerland and opened one of those special bank accounts with lots of numbers you can't remember, so no one else can either.

I toned down my high-style living, but it was too late.

I got a call from Robin Leach to appear on *Lifestyles of the Rich and Famous*. Great! How was I going to explain how I got so rich? I declined, saying I was too busy making money.

I went to my family doctor. "What's the problem?"

"I can't sleep, I'm getting tired of fancy restaurants where I can't pronounce the names of the foods that give me indigestion. Everywhere I go I feel like somebody's watching me and I've developed this twitch in my eye."

He sent me to a psychiatrist.

"You need some relaxation. Take a trip to the Bahamas and forget about your troubles."

"But doc, I don't have any troubles. I'm rich!"

"Why are you here then?"

I forgot, so I went home and took a sleeping pill.

"Wake up, wake up! Are you okay? What's the matter?"

I sprang forward in bed. It was my boss!

"What are you doing here, how did you get in my house?"

"You've never been late in seven years. You didn't answer the phone. We were worried. Your neighbor let me in."

I still had my job. Thank God. I didn't have to worry anymore about the IRS. The dream was over! I gave my lottery tickets away and promised myself I'd never again dream about being rich.

It was great to see Julia Roberts and Kim Bassinger lying seductively on my sofa waiting for me the next day when I got home. They were wearing nothing but . . .

Contemplating the Value of Books

Books. More books. And still more.

It's exhausting and frustrating when you have to load and unload boxes of books to make room for a new sofa.

As I sat on the floor sifting through them, I couldn't remember what most of them were about. Many of them were there to impress others and myself that I was well-read and knowledgeable.

I sat for a long time with these old bindings, staring at them and contemplating their true value.

I felt bad about insulting the authors by not reading what they had to say. I felt sad I was abandoning some old friends, donating them to a used book store where they might languish alone forever.

I felt guilty about those I borrowed and hadn't returned. And I smiled while reading a note from a friend on the inside front cover of *How to Get Rich*: "Forget it." How idealistic I was so long ago.

I held the tattered paperback of *The Godfather*. It was chewed on by Bear when he was a teething puppy. Tears flooded my eyes. He is old now, preferring soft slippers and newspapers.

Vivid memories of terror came back as I held *Psycho*. I remembered my reluctance to stay at an isolated motel in New Mexico when I was younger. I smiled wryly when holding the thick Economics I college textbook I kept around for restless nights when I couldn't sleep. Counting sheep couldn't help, but comparing apples and oranges usually did.

I placed a copy of the *Communist Manifesto* next to *Capitalism Today* and was glad I had learned most of my political values through real-life experiences, although I'm still confused.

Many self-help books reflected years of self-analysis. I'm still not sure who I am, but when I picked up *Winnie the Pooh*, I felt happy knowing that just "being" was okay.

There were books by Plato and Shakespeare and Ayn Rand. And there were those I *could* understand by Jules Verne, Mark Twain and Erma Bombeck. I didn't have any of those spicy romance novels, but I smiled again, holding copies of *Phantom of the Opera* and *How to Make Love to a Woman*. Neither had helped me much.

The true value of my books was revealed when I decided which to discard and which to keep.

I kept those borrowed in case someone I cared about asked me to return them. I kept the classics like *Origin of Species* and *The Rise and Fall of the Third Reich*. I couldn't read them because they were too long to be entertaining, but they looked impressive and filled a lot of space on the shelf next to Michener.

I threw out all the cookbooks and the mystery novels because I'm getting older — can't eat anything good anymore and life itself is more of a mystery than any story could be.

I saved the gift books I've never read strictly out of guilt, and the self-help books for a friend in need who might want more from me than I could offer. I saved novels made into movies, because the movies were never as good. But I cleared out those on how to write movies and novels because that fantasy had faded away when I learned it took too much work to succeed.

Perhaps we collect books because we outgrow bottle caps, old magazines, dolls, stuffed animals, family photos and baseball cards. They stay on shelves because they look nice, impress us and our friends, fill up vacant space in a room or cover cracks and scratches on the walls and dirty spots on the floor.

They help justify buying the bookcases that provide a place for knickknacks and bowling trophies.

We keep books to justify foolish expenditures when we thought we needed something to read in the sun, or to appear "well-read" so friends and neighbors could talk about us with some respect.

I felt foolish and a little depressed going through all those books. Curiosity, knowledge and vicarious adventures seemed so irrelevant when I had finished loading and carrying the heavy boxes.

It was sad.

My personal history and self-reflection the books stirred up were worth thinking about. Maybe I'd write my own book to put on a shelf someday.

At least I would be remembered when somebody bought a new sofa. At most, I might understand the contents.

Awkward Adolescence Akin to Aging Gracefully

Last week I stumbled off the 50-year-old starting blocks.

I believe I'm substantially wiser today than I was at 10, not much smarter than I was at 20, less naive than at 30 and more afraid than when I attained 40. I'm generally disappointed, though, that aging gracefully isn't all it's cracked up to be.

Being a half century old is an interesting conversation topic with people who have two minutes to spare. Turning 50 is a good opportunity for serious reflection if you're not busy indulging in important activities like criticizing politicians and celebrities you privately envy. And after five decades, it's discouraging to see your bank statement doesn't reflect the financial success of earlier dreams.

Since I don't know anyone who has two minutes to talk with me about this situation, I thought I'd share some significant observations about aging with readers like you who recognize how serious and significant this state of affairs really is.

I believe being 50 is similar to awkward adolescence. I remember feeling embarrassed about pimples and hair growing where it hadn't before, and now notice wrinkles and no hair where hair once was. I don't worry now what peers think about my clothes, but rather what fits and if they need to be ironed.

I rarely think about what I'm going to be when I grow up. I'm already grown up and still don't know what I am. When I was a teenager I wanted a '57 Ford Thunderbird but couldn't afford it. Now it's a classic. I still can't afford it. When a girl turned me down for a date in high school, I felt real bad. Now when I smile seductively at my wife and she says, "Sleep well," and turns on the TV instead of me, I feel relieved.

It was always fun dining out with my parents. I tried to act sophisticated but needed help to cut the steak properly with the right utensils. Now I worry whether dentures will fall out while chewing the steak, and thankfully need only a spoon for soups and ice cream. I once dreamed of being a baseball star like Mickey Mantle and still do — but now I dream of a no-cut, $20-million contract whether I can play or not. And I'm still as embarrassed today about my ineptness with Shakespeare as I was in school when I had to recite his words without knowing what they meant. "Ay, there's the rub," said Hamlet.

So here I sit, contemplating the significance of my life, comparing myself with parrots and tortoises and whales and wine and rocks and trees and people and other things, organic and inorganic — all half-century survivors. And the only commonality among us is that nothing really matters. Whatever we do will make little difference in the world. Just being is all there is. Except, of course, if you can play basketball, or program a VCR, or find cures for AIDS, cancer, politics, obesity and bad humor.

Just being isn't really so bad, though. I've survived a lot of self-inflicted and otherwise routine chaos in this unfair world and can still listen with some insight to dignitaries like Limbaugh and Stern. Even Beavis and Butthead say many of the same authoritative things my parents, friends and teachers said when I was younger. Nothing much has changed. I still like ice cream, going to the movies and playing violent games. (*I've traded my BB gun for a computer*). I still enjoy gawking at women who look the other way and bragging about imaginative athletic feats and big fish I never saw. Money, love, food and disagreeing about political issues I know nothing about, are still interesting subjects, too.

Yes, I'm a prematurely grumpy old man with a cynical attitude different than the idealism I proudly felt during my adolescent years. The difference, I hope, is that when I see youngsters wearing baseball hats backwards and talking about the importance of Haagen Dazs ice cream and pizza in a healthy diet, or when I watch young adults cramming for exams, talking about interesting tax deductions, discussing sex and marriage or MTV, now I'm able to laugh at myself for thinking I'm any smarter or less awkward than they.

I hope this accumulation of wisdom will guide me into the next era of personal growth with grace and courage and an even healthier sense of humor.

It's only when I look in a full-length mirror or lose an argument to a high school sophomore, that I realize this task won't be any easier than stumbling through the first 50 years.

PART FIVE:
If History Repeats Itself,
Why Can't We Stop It?

Balancing Logic with Emotion:
The Returns Are Worth It

Logical people make me crazy because they win arguments.

Emotional people make me crazy too, because they're just like me and I often can't understand them.

This is what makes tax time so frustrating.

"What do you mean?" I screamed at Charlie, my always logical tax consultant.

"You made too much this year," he said. "You owe taxes."

"Charlie! I need the money to pay for a psychiatrist. I'm going nuts trying to pay off those damn credit card bills and the loan on the new boat. And my wife's desperate for new clothes. Doesn't Uncle Sam have any compassion?"

"You're taking this too personally," said Charlie. "It's not an emotional issue. The numbers add up — you owe money. And your Uncle Sam is a fantasy figure," he explained, "just like Santa Claus, Superman and the Tooth Fairy."

"You're kidding, Charlie. I always thought Uncle Sam was real. So who do you call to get me a pardon on the money I owe?"

"I wish that were possible, but I can't. Listen. If you don't leave my office right away my wife is going to kill me for being late for dinner. She's a very emotional woman who doesn't like re-heating my food, especially when I have to explain that my clients get emotional about their taxes."

"I don't care *what* your wife thinks, Charlie! I'm paying you to make Uncle Sam *owe me*. And I bet your wife doesn't care what *you* think when you logically tell her she shouldn't get emotional just because you forgot to be at your daughter's ballet recital, the garbage disposal isn't working or you forgot your anniversary and haven't told her you love her for 16 years!"

Charlie was silent for a moment.

"Listen, buddy. Life is a logical system. You work, feed the family, keep a roof over your head and pay taxes. I tell my wife that all the time. After she screams a little, she agrees. So why are you giving me an emotional lecture about paying your taxes? Can't you see it's a simple, rational, matter-of-fact, make-sense proposition?"

"Hey, Charlie, I'm not arguing. If I agree with you and my other logical friends, that doesn't mean I can't be emotional. Logic has its place in science and law, but how in the world does it work when you're late for work and get a flat tire, the hot water heater breaks when it's time to shower, your 15-year-old daughter starts crying when you tell her she can't have a new car, or you get the flu on the first day of a Hawaiian vacation?"

Charlie and I discussed logic and emotion for two hours. He became very frustrated. He worried what his wife was going to say when he got home, and how far behind he was in his work.

"I can't take it anymore!" he screamed. "I gotta get outa here, now! How did I ever let you get me started on this ridiculous discussion. It doesn't make any sense! And I can't bill you for this time! It's not logical."

Charlie was beginning to make me crazy being so emotional.

He showed me to the door, which he slammed behind both of us as we went our separate ways.

Two weeks later I received my tax return. Charlie didn't let me down. He was brilliant and creative. I didn't owe any taxes!

Attached was a note.

"Thanks for making me emotional. I was so angry when I got home late because of you, I screamed at my whole family. My kids and wife have never seen me that way before. They were very logical and supportive. They understood my feelings. I was surprised. My wife smiled when I didn't eat my re-heated dinner. I felt great letting it all out. I even called my partner and told him I

wasn't coming in and he could do all the work. My wife and I are on a vacation to be emotional together. Thanks, Charlie."

I was happy for him. I looked over my tax return carefully and noted deductions of $2,500 for charities I had never heard of. The $8,500 in medical expenses were off by $8,000.

Charlie lost his logic, and perhaps his career. Dianna is now my new accountant.

Tax time is a good opportunity to balance logic with emotion. The returns are well worth the effort.

All Thumbs Up for Future Academy Awards

The Academy Awards.

What have we got this year? Well, Clint Eastwood has finally earned recognition for creative facial stubble and filthy violence. He turned down commercial offerings from Gillette, spitting cigar juice in the faces of the ad men who suggested Right Guard instead of razors.

We've got Al Pacino up for best actor in *Scent of a Woman*, and he, like Eastwood, was also offered a job he *did* refuse — Chanel No.5 ads. *A Few Good Men* is nominated. Jack Nicholson, not one of those good men, got nominated anyway because he scared Academy voters as well as audiences.

And no tears will be shed if best picture nominee, *The Crying Game*, loses, unless your own partner had a sex-change operation.

So here we go with my annual offerings — *great* movies you should see which Hollywood hasn't even *thought* of yet — my annual revenge against the moguls who rejected my script for *Breaking Wind* several years ago when I was aspiring to be rich and famous.

The Numbers Game — Tom Cruise stars as a respected accountant bribed by an angry ex-IRS agent (Gene Hackman). Hackman loses his job when it's discovered he cheated on his taxes, and now wants Cruise to re-work the numbers, making it appear he is *owed* money by the IRS so he can get his job back. He's caught again, wins a prison term at a closed-down military base in Honolulu, escapes to California and wins the Lottery. He pays a bundle to Cruise, who turns out to be a crooked IRS investigator.

Vultures From Outer Space VII — Alien dinosaur eggs hatch aboard *Starship Tyrannosaurus*. The little creatures escape after landing on Earth. Remains of the crew grow mysteriously into giant skeletal monsters who stalk the planet in search of their parents.

Butch Takes A Holiday — The true story of a teenage boy who steals his father's pick-up truck to smuggle potatoes from Idaho to Nebraska. He gets involved with a Cornhusker farmer's daughter. She's really from Texas and is developing a new oil-drilling technique to drain crude from Montana to Nebraska and sell it in Tennessee. As the plot thickens, the romance becomes very sticky when oil gets mysteriously clogged in the pipeline.

The Laundry Chronicles — Set in a southern Florida town, this romantic comedy revolves around four couples who meet weekly in a laundromat. They become engaged in rotating romances and starchy arguments. A big-screen soap opera, this turbulent and dirty film explores the frustrations of getting soaked sipping too many suds and ironing out interpersonal miscommunication.

It's A Dog's Life — A film centered on the life of the slovenly, bumbling dog-catcher Johnny Milkbone, (Rodney Dangerfield), who is bitten severely by a pit bull and dies. Johnny is reincarnated as a poodle. While taking a walk he's arrested by the new dog-catcher in town. He's put into a home for lost dogs with no respect. There he meets Fifi. Still getting no respect, his sexual advances are refused by Fifi and a violent battle ensues. The hair-raising climax proves it's easier to be a friend than a dog.

Rocky Meets Rambo — A sensitive story about two macho warriors who, upon meeting each other for the first time, discover they like each other. They learn gentle love and become teachers at an orphanage. When a drug-dealer tries to use the home for a hideout, the two return to their violent ways. They take out the dealer and go to Colombia where they annihilate the entire drug trade, leaving behind massive environmental destruction and anarchy. The shocking, graphic climax finds the two loving each other — a lot.

The Last Jazzman — A politically-charged thriller examines a mysterious malady that afflicts the U.S. president. He becomes seriously ill but can't get treated because his budget adviser has over-zealously cut the health-care budget. The president disappears. He's later found homeless in New Orleans playing saxophone for quarters in a wild, uncontrolled manner. A hoax? A billionaire computer tycoon thinks so. He's secretly networking PC's and video cameras nearby. Television crews are standing by for exclusive reports.

Nintendo Master — A family sci-fi movie about 9-year-old Billy Wipple. This lovable genius devises a scheme to get even with his anti-nerd tormentors at school. Using his father's powerful Pentium computer, Billy creates graphic look-alike images of his adversaries and downloads the data into his Super Nintendo game. He plays out his fantasies using devastating weaponry and martial arts techniques. The adventure begins when all of his friends want to be heroes on the magical screen. But something goes wrong and . . .

Take *that*, Hollywood!

To win free tickets to these future classics, call someone who cares and pick the one(s) you'd most like to see. When the votes are tallied, you will be contacted and asked for $10 million to help finance the movie(s) of your choice.

If you choose to invest, find a good psychiatrist.

Advice — Don't Take It If You Don't Use It

I've always envied advice gurus like Abby, Landers, Dr. Ruth and teenagers. They all have answers for everything.

Like most people, however, I hear lots of it but rarely use it. Perhaps that's why I do this rather than making a living as a Little League umpire or ice-cream truck driver.

ADVENTURES IN THE SLOW LANE

Their advice on what to do in serious situations is very helpful. For example, coping when toilet paper runs out after you've excused yourself from a big meal at a new friend's house; or quieting shotgun-toting neighbors settling quarrels in their backyards when you're trying to sleep; or choosing an ensemble for a formal White House dinner when you're strictly K-Mart; or understanding simple subjects like world economics and military strategy; and why marrying a nymphomaniac if you're over 60 is a healthy life-style alternative to Geritol and exercise bikes.

These and other trivial issues have inspired me to write a *serious* advice column — against the counsel of good friends.

Following is advice to a few of the forlorn I've enlightened just for practice. Under the Freedom of Folly Act, this information is being published without fear of censorship or retribution.

Dear Gary: I'm feeling ashamed. Everyone's been writing bad things about me. I'm really a swell guy. Nobody sees the good and romantic side of me. How can I change my image? HELPLESS IN BAGHDAD.

Dear Saddam: Shake hands and give George Bush a hug. Go hunt with him — birds instead of people. Follow carefully his election campaign strategy when you return home and run for president using the democratic process. Good luck!

Dear Gary: I'm urgently faxing you from my dressing room in Bangkok. I'm terrified to appear in public tonight, especially around children, because of all this negative publicity. What should I do? EXHAUSTED ON TOUR.

Dear Michael: Wear gloves on both hands, get rid of the leather, stop grabbing your crotch when you perform and don't sing songs like *Beat It, Bad* and *Thriller*. Most people know your devotion to children is sincere and wonderful. Sing safe songs like *I Wanna Be Free, I'm Just a Lonely Boy* and *My Way*. Play it straight for awhile. Let the issue blow over.

Dear Gary: I'm a housewife in Alaska where it's always pretty cold. My husband says I'm frigid, but I think it's just the weather. We have six kids which proves I'm not prudish, but he wants to do it all the time; mostly when I'm cleaning fish or thawing out the laundry. How much sex is normal under these severe conditions? CAUGHT IN THE COLD.

Dear Cold: I don't know. But your husband sounds like a weirdo. Write to Dr. Ruth.

Dear Gary: I felt terrible reading that letter from the woman whose husband tries to be macho. She claims he doesn't take showers or shave, wears dirty clothes, doesn't talk to her when she's upset and says *make my day* while pointing squirt guns at her when she threatens to leave him. Should I accept responsibility for this behavior? UNFORGIVEN.

Dear Clint: It's unfortunate you've become a role model for violence and intimidation. Continue focusing on your strong points, like when you were mayor of Carmel and made it legal to buy ice cream after dark and on Sundays.

Dear Gary: Every time I eat out with my husband, he slurps his coffee, holds spaghetti up and lowers it, full-length into his big mouth, wipes his face on the table cloth if he drops his napkin and then leaves me with the check while he goes to the bar for an after-meal drink. What should I do to teach him better manners? DISGUSTED.

Dear Disgusted: Invite Dr. Kevorkian over for dinner. Your husband will get the message.

Dear Gary: What can I say to my girl who left me for my best friend? HURTING IN TEXAS.

Dear Hurting: She's not your girl anymore — say nothing. Get drunk and eat a bowl of hot chili and onions. Say something to him up close, *very* close. Then determine why he was better than you, take some drugs and sleep it off. Go find another friend with bad taste and get another girl. Don't worry, be realistic.

Dear Gary: When I finish college I want to be a great columnist like you. I want the big bucks and fame. I want to write brilliant commentaries on all worldly topics. Do you have suggestions on how to accomplish my dream? ADMIRER.

Dear Admirer: First, get off the drugs. Then see a psychiatrist. Drop the dream, kid. Get a job in Alabama building good cars or become a Little League umpire. Be happy. With some luck and *good* advice, you'll get both!

A Gas of a Super Bowl, Full of Beans

The Gulf War enriched the strategic thinking of mankind.

Saddam Hussein gave us the indelible "Mother of all battles," a quote as memorable as Clint Eastwood's "Make my day," George Bush's "Read my lips," General Powell's "Cut it off and kill it," and Arnold Schwarzenegger's "Hasta la vista, baby!" Guys who talk as eloquently as this make excellent coaches and commentators.

So let's put other talk aside and get on with America's *real* concern — the Super Bowl.

Coaches Hussein for Buffalo and Powell for Washington, were last seen shaking hands at a foreign-aid, fund-raising dinner in Russia, their last stop on a promotional tour for the new Super Bowl sponsor — Jeep's personal 4x4 armored vehicle.

Meanwhile analysts Arnold, Clint and George were preparing for the game in a bunker on Miami Beach, drawing lines in the sand while drinking Gatorade moonshine brewed in the Everglades. Their conversation was taped by a CNN reporter burrowed in the sand, who had, without authorization, left the press pool at the hotel.

182

ARNOLD — "Boys, I think Hussein's forces will dig in and play tough defense. They have all their big gorillas on the front line. They'll sacrifice them to ease the burden on the defensive backs preparing for Washington's strong air attack."

GEORGE — "Good point, Arnold, but let's be prepared for the unexpected. Powell might mount a diversionary air attack to feign superiority while the Washington quarterback is recovering from that arm-wrestling contest he lost to you at the press dinner the other night. He might use his end sweeps like he did in the real war."

CLINT — "No way, fellas. Washington will run right up the middle, using up the clock so the instant replay cameras can work longer to give the sponsors more air time. Remember, the game is being shown in 123 countries. The owners need the bucks to grease some political palms. It's an election year."

GEORGE — "Do you think the coaches will use dirty tricks?

ARNOLD — "It's Astroturf, so Hussein will probably spill the Gatorade on the field to make footing difficult. I heard he's filled some footballs with gas to make them go farther when Buffalo goes to the air. If a ball gets thrown into the stands it could blow up in a smoker's face, causing the crowd to get more involved in the battle."

CLINT — "That's possible, but not probable. I spoke to one of the Buffalo tackles. He told me Hussein was feeding them a special diet of Kurdish meatballs, imported Jordanian rice and a secret recipe of 14-bean soup. An army crawls on its stomach. I think the gas attack is inevitable and Powell should be preparing for a strong ground game — downwind."

GEORGE — "It doesn't matter what Hussein is planning. Powell has prepared better. He's requisitioned gas-retardant face-mask helmets equipped with heat-seeking, infra-red ball-finders. Each coach has a computer system linking the press box and each player's helmet. But the team that can operate its radar jammers most effectively will disrupt their opponent's command."

ARNOLD — "But George, isn't that illegal in football?"

183

GEORGE — "All's fair in love and war, pal, and I don't think the American people will tolerate a Super Bowl that's like another Vietnam. Somebody's gotta win big. Hell, what will we do at game-time if we can't use modern warfare? What will we have gained from the strategy learned in Iraq? Now that Russia's not a threat, this Super Bowl is *everything* to any warrior worth his broccoli."

ARNOLD — "I hope those engineers will finish the prototype T-1993 Terminator in time for next year's game. Can you imagine a running back who can't be stopped, a quarterback who throws a football the length of the field, a field-goal kicker who kicks 100-yarders or a crunched-up lineman that can say, 'I'll be back?' "

CLINT — "I like it! To hell with strategy. I'd love to see a defensive back decapitate a split-end. It would really make my day!"

GEORGE — "Well fellas, read my lips. Quoting my favorite statesman, this is going to be one helluva *mother of all battles.* Barbara and I are looking forward to welcoming the winning team to the White House for dinner. Of course, if it's Buffalo, we'll have to ask the coach to come at a later date. It's an election year, you know. But my guess is it will be Washington. I think the score will be 49-0."

ARNOLD — "Do you know something we don't, George?"

GEORGE — "Could be!"

CLINT — "It's always the same. Every time I play *Dirty Harry* I have to fight the establishment as much as the criminals. Why can't this game be just among the players?"

ARNOLD — "Marketing, my friend, marketing! Money, money, money! I know this stuff. I'm so pumped up and excited about my first game analysis, I even signed on to promote a new deodorant called Stuporscent. I'm wearing it right now. Wanna smell?"

CLINT — "This whole event stinks. I don't care who wins or loses. This game gets more attention than Christmas or my birthday."

GEORGE — "Let's get going. I've gotta get to the stadium before Powell and Hussein. There are some great photo ops for me. I just hope no one finds out I wouldn't let Reagan announce the game."

Planning a Politically Correct Vacation

White House travel staff members were fired.

I guess they shouldn't have arranged so many adventurous vacations for politicians to Somalia, Iraq, Haiti and Cleveland. Even at taxpayer expense, these unusual ventures must have caused a lot of confusion at the IRS.

This firing in the Capitol, however, caused me to seriously question the judgment of my own travel agent, Herbert Hipple. Last year I asked for an easy-going, inexpensive trip where I could relax and do nothing. Herbie sent me to Nothing, Arizona, on a Greyhound Bus. There was no golf course, no swimming pool, no fishing, no cable TV and no bar. I got just what I asked for — nothing except an overdose of boredom.

This year will be different.

"How ya doin' Herbie?" I smiled when I entered the disheveled office in his cabin by the river. "Now *that's* a big fish," I said pointing at the photo on the wall of a fisherman with his catch.

"Oh, that's Willie Mumford. Sent him up to Alaska last winter. Booked him on the train, then a private plane, then on a dog sled to this secluded lake I know."

I didn't notice any snow in the picture.

"So what can we do for you this year?" he asked.

"Well, Herbie, Nothing was real nice last year, but this year I've got to do *something* exciting."

"Ya got big bucks?"

"No, but I'm willing to spend more than the $150 Wheel & Deal Special we tried last year for Nothing."

"Somethin' classy, right? Nice hotel, pool, Jacuzzi, entertainment, scenery, good food and reasonably priced?"

"Yeah."

"You're lucky. Just got a call from one of my associates in Geneva, Nebraska. They've got a one-time offer going this year. The recession, you know. For $1,200 you get a rental pick-up, large room at Motel 6, and four rounds of golf at the Geneva Country Club. This price, of course, includes admission to the annual International Hog-calling Festival and round-trip airfare to Winner, South Dakota for the National Square Dance Finals."

"Gee, Herbie, my wife and I would prefer something a bit more adventurous."

"No problem. Just got this new promotional package from an associate in Miami. It's a little dangerous, it's exciting — did this gig myself 18 years ago — for only $2,400 you get round trip airfare on a reconstructed Pan Am 747 and . . ."

"Whoa, Herbie! They're out of business."

"Not *this* plane. Me and two buddies bought it and refurbished it ourselves for charters only. No frills, but we serve croissants and that French bottled water stuff. Very quaint.

"Anyway, when you get down to Miami, you'll get a private guide. He'll take you to the Everglades where you'll get two days of canoe training. And don't worry about the alligators. After your six-hour wrestling lessons, you'll have no problem making your first pair of shoes and a lovely purse for your wife."

"You're kidding!"

"Nope. We hire only the best craftsman for this trip. If you survive, you'll have three days at the Miami Hilton to recuperate. Then it's off to . . ."

"Herbie, I think I need to review my vacation options. Can I call in a couple days?"

"Well, you can try. Business has been so brisk the phone company is installing two new lines so I can book more cheap flights. Airlines are getting desperate for passengers, you know."

"Sure."

I smiled, glancing at another photo showing a happy couple dancing in a ballroom where a tuxedoed orchestra appears to be playing romantic music. I noticed the touched-up edges where the couple had been not-so-carefully inserted.

I went home to do some thinking.

"Hello, Nancy. I'm calling to know if Motel 0 is available in September. We'd like to stop by for a visit. Taking the kid to

Disneyland and Sea World, but we're most anxious to see you and Richard. Is your extra room still available?"

"We'd love to see you. But it will cost a \$1. We've installed air-conditioning and a piped-in stereo system."

"Hello, Derek. Wondering if we could spend a couple nights with you and Juanita in September. Would love to play golf with you. Great. Looking forward to it."

"Hello, Dave. It's your daughter's birthday in September. We thought it would be nice to visit. Can we stay with you a couple nights? Thought we could all go out to a play. Good. See you then."

"Hi Ron. This is your brother. We'd like to visit you in September. Kinda tight on cash now. Any problem staying with you a couple nights? Great. No. Just haven't had time to call. Been busy this year." I lied. I can't stand my brother, but he has a big house.

"Well, honey. Our trip to Los Angeles is taken care of. Got places to stay and things to do. And best of all, we won't need the credit cards or a loan."

"What about Herbie?"

"Oh, he's doing great. Just got hired by Clinton to replace the travel agents in Washington. I'm sure he'll keep those politicians in the country where they belong and save the taxpayers a bundle."

No More Taxes for "Family, Inc."

I just returned from Dianna's place.

She does our taxes at the last minute for no extra charge in her tax-deductible home office. This was the second trip. The first was depressing. We owed \$3,000.

I'm smiling now, because we owe *nothing*! The government owes *us* \$4,000! We're talking to a travel agent now about using the refund as a deductible expense on next year's taxes — for a mental health-care trip to Hawaii.

187

I think I've discovered a way to stimulate the economy without paying taxes.

It's quite simple . . .

"Hi, Dianna," I said. "It's good to see you this time. After I got home knowing I owed $3,000, I couldn't sleep. Even with extra cheating, there's no way we could reduce *that* debt. Can we go over my new plan now?"

"Sure."

I placed the document on the desk. It read *"Schwartz Family, Inc., A Corporation."*

She looked at me incredulously with raised eyebrows.

"Looked the word 'business' up in the dictionary," I said. "No problem. We meet the requirements for a small business, so we incorporated. Yep, the kid is out delivering papers, the gardener is maintaining the plants, the cleaning lady is tidying up the executive kitchen and my wife is shopping for food and clothes.

"See, it's right there. Five employees, including the chief executive officer. Salaries are deductible. So is maintenance of plant and equipment. Yep, we're looking forward to deducting the new roof, paving the driveway and adding that other office where I can figure out more deductions. Infrastructure, you know!"

"What are you doing?" said Dianna. This isn't legal, is it?"

"Don't know. But Mr. Clinton is encouraging the growth of small businesses and I can't think why a family household shouldn't be considered a business, can you?

"Now, here are deductions for our cat, two dogs, two parakeets and the squirrel who eats the walnuts off our tree. Let's see, that makes six who depend on us for more than 50 percent of their existence. Yeah. Six dependents.

"As you can see here, Dianna, there were nine shopping trips for new clothes my wife needed so she'd look good at work and get raises. Uniforms, I figure. Twenty-eight movies we saw, deductible as preventive mental health care. I didn't include the popcorn and soft drinks. That would be going too far.

"Here are our deductions for utilities: garbage collection, water, electricity, clogged toilet repairs, vending machines . . ."

"Whoa! Vending machines?"

"Oh. We figured the frig, coffee maker and cupboard space for the cookies and chips should be deductible just like vending machines at factories and offices. You know, employee benefits!"

Dianna closed her eyes.

"Let's see now. Employee business transportation deductions. Yes. Gasoline, insurance, tires, tune-ups and car washes. Bicycle maintenance for the kid to get to school and for his paper route.

"Newspaper, magazine and cable TV subscriptions. Employee education deductions. Savings and investments, employee retirement and fringe benefit deductions."

"I can't take this anymore," screamed Dianna. "You can't expect me to go along with this crazy scheme? Do you really think the IRS will approve these deductions?"

"Sure Dianna. Look, if every family did the same, *shop 'til you drop* would have new meaning. Buy the most expensive clothes, the best tools for the farm, the strongest and most advanced pick-up. The more you spend, the more deductions. Spend or save as much as you make, and you owe no taxes. If you have a profit, then you pay 50 percent in tax. And *that* will be a *deduction* for charitable contributions to the government!

"With this incredible Spend and Deduct Plan, the recession will be over so quickly the government could take a year off."

"Where will the government get the money it needs to pay for all of *its* expenses?"

"Well, if you noticed, we didn't write off any deductions for our mortgage interest, so the IRS will save big there. Then, as you see here, I've added a 2 percent sales tax on everything we bought. That goes to the government."

"I think you're a little off-the-wall."

"Exactly. Another deduction for mental health expenses."

"I don't really think I can figure your taxes for you under these circumstances. You might reconsider and pay the $3,000 or get another accountant. I can't afford to go to jail for tax fraud."

"But Dianna, can't you see? *Everybody* will need a tax accountant to figure out their taxes. It can get so complicated. We need your expertise. See here," I said, pointing to a circle at the bottom of the page.

"I included legal deductions, just like big businesses and politicians do. I'll need legal help to defend my new tax plan. And there is a *huge* deduction for the tax preparer. *Real huge!*"

"Come back tomorrow. I'll see what I can do."

Like I said, it's quite simple. Owning your own business and getting tax breaks isn't just for the rich. The average American family deserves a break too!

Nobody's Fool Would Watch This Pulp Fiction

The Academy Awards, like life, are unjust.

There are few winners, and most great talents go unnoticed.

Me, for example. I was born in Hollywood. I tried to be an over-paid screenwriter with all the trimmings — beach house, Ferrari, extensive wardrobe of questionable taste and tax deductions for location research trips to hazardous places like Tahiti and Acapulco. I still haven't won an Academy Award after decades of effort and pain. So, to vent my disappointment once again, I want those ungrateful producers to know about their missed opportunities.

The Galloping Gourmand: Brandon, a Texas rodeo star of questionable intelligence (Jack Nicholson), breaks his back while trying to stand up on a bucking Brahma bull to win bonus money. He gains 78 pounds eating ribs and chili while recovering. Unable to make a living riding a bull, he decides to sling it instead. With his horse, Cannonball, he tours the world promoting his innovative cookbook, *The Galloping Gourmand.*

He prepares unusual food on TV and comments on irrational eating habits, then rides backwards on Cannonball shouting out his culinary philosophies. "Cajuns bite off crayfish heads and suck brains; this improves their intelligence. Californians drink too much of their own wine; that's why they fantasize about *legmeisters* Luigi and Guido who make unwanted visits to those buying Domino's Pizza instead of the Godfather's. The French eat snails to slow themselves down so they have more time to drink wine."

The plot? Brandon marries the beautiful Tina (Julia Roberts), who secretly desires to own the *Jenny Craig Weight-Loss Program.* She steals Brandon's fortune from book sales to buy in. When Brandon finds out, he must give up eating and lose weight or lose Tina. Is Brandon really stupid?

Doctor, Doctor, I Feel Your Pain: Supershrink Sylvia Childs (Barbra Streisand) sets up an emergency clinic in Scarsville, Missouri, where the whole town has fallen into a depressive state. After interviewing several people, Sylvia discovers the cause. "My husband," says a young woman, "watched the *Montel Williams Show* on 'Men who cheat for money'; he took up with a movie star." "My wife," says a young man, "was on the *Jenny Jones Show* about 'Women who marry for companionship'; but she dumped me for a guy who has a job."

During an investigation of the Supershrink, the depressed sheriff who has been a recent guest on the *Phil Donahue Show,* "Impotent men in uniform," discovers Sylvia is a producer for *60 Minutes,* investigating talk-show fraud. He arrests her for *shrinking* without a license. Stimulated by the experience, his potency returns. His wife is grateful. He then shouts to 36 depressed citizens moping around town, "I feel your pain, I feel your pain, have some of mine!" He opens fire on them with an AK47.

ADVENTURES IN THE SLOW LANE

Honey, You're Driving Me Crazy: Roger (Eddie Murphy) and Becky (Whoopi Goldberg) are having marital problems. They take a driving vacation from San Francisco to Connecticut. The auto lights fail; they crash into a telephone pole. The heater fails; they're in the hospital with frostbite. Two tires blow out in the desert; they're hospitalized with heat stroke. The windshield wipers malfunction; they get stuck in a mud hole in a rainstorm and are hospitalized with pneumonia. The brakes fail; they slam into a fire hydrant. He blames her. "Every time you use the car, something goes wrong." They finally arrive in Connecticut. He gets a speeding ticket and is arrested for driving without insurance or valid registration. "And you never pay the insurance bill on time."

They divorce. He becomes a used car salesman; she, a surgeon. Now good friends, they start a travel agency. He rents junkers, she repairs the drivers.

I Was A Teenage Tax Evader: Tommy (Michael J. Fox) is running for president of the United States. Just before the primaries, his best friend from junior high school, Matt (Matt Dillon) turns him in to the IRS for reward money. Tommy is investigated for income tax evasion. He didn't declare income from paper routes, chores, lemonade stands, garage sales, birthday and Christmas gifts, baseball and basketball card sales, allowances and Sega Game contests. He wins the election anyway. Revenge is sweet. Matt is turned down for tickets to the Inauguration and is arrested for crashing the party. Tommy persuades Congress to pass new IRS regulations giving substantial tax deductions to parents who prove their children know how to make and save money.

Still hopeful there may be justice in the world, I've got my Academy acceptance speech ready and waiting. It's as good as my movie ideas. If you'd like to hear it, contact a producer you might know and tell him to make one of these movies.

If not, I'll accept my fate instead of the award. I have a speech ready for that occasion too. It's titled: *I'm nobody's fool. Life is a bowl of pulp fiction.*

Personalities Deter(mine) Super Bowl Atmosphere

It's party time!

The Super Bowl, once again! America gets a three-and-a-half-hour respite from life's agonies — unless, of course, your mother-in-law is visiting Sunday and squawks about the house filled with disgusting smoke, snacks and strangers.

The personalities of the commentators determine Super Bowl atmosphere as much as the teams. Last year, you'll recall, Saddam Hussein, on leave of absence from his military command, had an opportunity to exhibit his combat strategy coaching the ground-pounding Buffalo Bills against Colin Powell who managed the air attack of the winning Washington Redskins.

It was a one-sided game, and the macho male commentators George Bush, Arnold Schwarzenegger and Clint Eastwood enjoyed their duties providing expert commentary.

Now, with a new administration, there's a different atmosphere for the game.

Ross Perot is coaching the Dallas Cowboys, and the Buffalo Bills are under the spell of Jerry Brown.

Barbara Bush, as part of her new job, will gracefully receive the smiles and waves of the players as the official, *Hi, Mom!*

David Letterman and Jay Leno are judges for the new Touchdown Dance and Spike Contest. And commentators Miss Manners and Oprah Winfrey are in the press box preparing for the big game. *(Dr. Ruth declined at the last minute. She was stimulating her husband to study football's new fore-play).*

193

MANNERS: "This is quite a spectacle. I wonder why the players like so much violence. It just isn't necessary."

OPRAH: "They need to demonstrate their physical prowess to prove their manhood. But it's interesting they hid from me in the locker room, dressed only in their cute little jockeys. I think they were embarrassed to be seen up close by a woman other than their mother."

MANNERS: "Well, I think this game would be more pleasant if the contestants restrained themselves from patting each other on those jockeys and spitting as they do. And those awful obscenities! The referees should blow the whistle and stop the game when a player goes wild like that."

OPRAH: "That would be difficult and perhaps socially irresponsible. I talked with Bobby Blockhead of the Bills. He says knocking a guy down in a game stops him from killing people in the streets. But then, on the other hand, I talked to Jerry Brown. He's stressing non-violence. He's coached his team to meditate for 20 seconds in the huddles and then chant just before the snap. He said this will build team spirit and psych-out the Cowboys."

MANNERS: "That's so nice. Unfortunately, I heard from my hairdresser that Ross has drilled his players with a no-nonsense, all-business technique. No huddles to discuss strategy. 'Just do it,' he said, 'until you drop.' They'll discuss strategy at half-time. Of course, if they're losing, Ross might disappear for awhile, then reappear if he sees a chance to win."

OPRAH: "That's Ross, all right!"

MANNERS: "The game sets a poor example. I'm concerned those dirty uniforms and bloody bandages will encourage youngsters watching to be careless about their personal hygiene and health. And those cheerleaders! It's disgraceful to use sex to sell tickets."

OPRAH: "The players are just big kids doing what comes naturally. Mad-Dog McGurk, the Dallas guard, told me confidentially that he always wanted to grow up to be a cowboy. Cowboys get dirty. And a little sex *does* work. Those guys have nice buns. Just look at those classic, sculptured hardbodies.

"Listen, I'd like you on my show next week. Magic Johnson and Joe Namath are guests for 'Women who love athletes, and the athletes who can't ignore them.' You can talk to them about better manners. The following week I'm having Ross and Jerry on the show to discuss their game strategies. Ross is encouraging his players to *kick butt* to earn lots of extra Super Bowl money, and Jerry is telling them to accept only $1 to support lower ticket prices."

MANNERS: "Damn! (Oops, sorry), but I'm afraid I'll have to decline your offer. I wouldn't feel comfortable in such a combative atmosphere. I don't know if I could be polite for an entire hour."

OPRAH: "Why aren't we talking more about the game? We're getting paid to comment on the game, not to gossip as usual."

MANNERS: "Good point. Can we pick our favorites before the contest begins? I don't know much about football."

OPRAH: " I pick the Bills. Jerry Brown can *buffalo* anyone into thinking they can win."

MANNERS: "That's funny, Oprah. And I'll pick the Cowboys because Perot can throw the bull and do the *two-step* better than anyone. I think he'll inspire his players to do the same."

Enough! I'd rather put up with my mother-in-law and all her squawking, than listen to this nonsense.

Let the violence begin and the beer flow! Get the bets down and let the touchdown dances be plentiful!

We all need a short respite from the world's problems.

A Misadventure in Vacation Planning

As you know, visiting my eccentric travel agent Herbert Hipple is an adventure I look forward to every June. At 78 he still has youthful enthusiasm for inventive vacation ideas, although he may be losing some of the edge he once had over the competition.

I pulled up alongside his cabin on the river. He was plucking weeds with chopsticks between planks of his porch steps.

"How ya doing Herbie?" I asked. "How's business?"

"Not too good. Been spending more time fishing than working since I lost my job at the White House."

"What happened?"

"They didn't care much for my no-frills vacations; complained I didn't understand the complex uses of helicopters, military jets and computerized travel analyses. I think I embarrassed them too, refusing to shed my coveralls for a suit."

"That's all?"

"Well, I guess it wasn't too smart of me to skip lunch with Robin Leach. They said it was part of the government's re-training program for the socially deprived. I didn't think his influence would change my attitude any."

"Well, Herbie, we certainly enjoyed your plan for us to visit friends in Los Angeles last year. The minimal cost of the T-shirts with *Manager, Motel 0* printed on them brought grateful smiles to our hosts' faces who understood our financial plight. They had no idea we spent a fortune at theme parks, thought we were looking for quarters on the beach every day."

"Yeah. That's one of the most popular features of my vacation plans." He pointed at a wall map of the United States where pins were stuck in several places.

"I personally never spend a dime on accommodations, very little on eating out," he smiled devilishly. "Friends are always flattered that I'd rather spend a vacation with them in small towns than in the Bahamas or Bora Bora. I play golf, go fishing and get in some serious poker and drinking. I'm especially fond of the friends

196

I've cultivated who live conveniently near natural playgrounds like Yellowstone, Yosemite, Grand Canyon and Las Vegas."

"Your knowledge must have been useful in Washington. What went wrong there?"

"Those people have *too many* friends; I couldn't keep up with their schedules or understand their tastes."

"For example?"

"Well, there's this woman senator from Washington who wears tennis shoes a lot and lives close to where they make them. She was speaking at a fund-raiser at the shoe factory, then wanted to go on a personal Alaskan vacation with a Native American friend."

"So?"

"I found her a low-cost junket that goes up the coast of Washington and doesn't use government transportation. It was politically and environmentally correct."

"Great!"

"I thought so too, but she was concerned about not being back in the Capitol when Congress reconvened."

"I don't understand."

"The canoe trip takes four months."

"Then I planned an inexpensive golf excursion for two Secret Service agents. They were really angry at me when I booked them at an exclusive golf resort in Israel."

"Why was that?"

"They were asked to leave on the eighth hole."

"Why?"

"I got them free carts and green fees on the premise they were supposed to be checking security for a possible Clinton visit the next month. But I forgot to tell them that. They got stuck in a sand trap and arrested for drunk driving and bragging loudly about their scores at private courses in Paris and Geneva."

"Sorry about your misfortune, Herbie. But we'd still like your help — something more exciting this year."

"Got just the thing. You can stay at a grand hotel with a friend in Washington D.C. and spend your money on some really different experiences. The whole trip can be written off as a tax deduction because you'll be doing important research."

"Sounds interesting. Go on."

"Yep. You'll have to pay cash up front, but I can arrange government helicopter and limo rides anywhere you want to go — maybe a trip on Air Force One with triple frequent flyer miles. And I think I can even throw in a private dinner with the president."

"Wow! Who will we be staying with?"

"Robin Leach. He's doing an undercover, documentary TV special on soon-to-be rich and infamous Capitol insiders."

"I thought you snubbed him?"

"I did. Only faked it though. We were working together. We're old friends. Met him 45 years ago when I was learning the business in North Dakota. Wouldn't want those politicos to know an old, wretched, socially-deprived travel agent was taking them for the ride of their lives, now, would we?"

"But Herbie, how am I going to get rich and infamous?"

"Easy. With the information I give you, you'll find lots of new, influential friends there willing to substantially increase your standard of living, just to keep themselves out of the book you'll write after your vacation trip."

"Herbie, you're incorrigible."

"Yep. Also a brilliant agent who knows how to uncover a lot of simple and interesting travel secrets." Amen.

Desperate People Want To Know

Since I wrote my first advice column a few months ago, many questionably intelligent readers have requested more guidance.

Although advice only bolsters what you believe already, and nobody can change your mind about what you think, unless you don't think, which is a good reason not to ask for advice and also not to read run-on, rambling sentences like this one, which is good advice, because I really don't have anything important to say anyway.

However, if you've gotten this far and you're still interested, I'll provide some of the significant letters and responses so you can advise me if I should continue writing advice columns.

———

Dear Gary: I'm concerned about what I should wear to this week's special occasion. I'd like to maintain some dignity when I step down, but I'm not sure khakis and knee-high boots are appropriate protective gear in case of monsoons or ambush when I leave the palace. Please advise. LONELY IN HAITI.

Dear Lonely: Fashionable wear for ousters and resignations by despotic rulers includes sharkskin coveralls by Pardalucci, a pigskin face mask by Romanoski with matching rat-skin gloves and footwear by Turagammo. If you survive the laughter, then run like hell for the nearest river and hope your Gucci swim wear will protect you from the other snakes.

Dear Gary: My wife has threatened to volunteer both of us for the *Montel Williams Show*, 'Women who love men who love themselves and not women.' Although it's flattering that she thinks I would make good fodder for television viewers, I believe I'm too good-looking, well-built and intelligent to be on Montel's moronic show. I'd prefer *Oprah, Donahue* or *Larry King*. I'd like to tell her she can go on by herself because I don't give a damn what she does, as long as it's good for me. But if she goes on Montel's show, it will cause me great embarrassment. What can I say to her so she doesn't? BARRY IN BALTIMORE.

Dear Barry: Tell her you're taking a restorative vacation in Bosnia to reflect on life and humility and won't be available for observation on *any* show until further notice. When you leave, take along a tiny pocket mirror for your daily reflection exercises. May God have mercy on your soul.

Dear Gary: I'm becoming alarmed and extremely annoyed by several hundred lookey-loos who come by every day to stare at my next door neighbor's place from my front yard. Although at first I enjoyed the attention, it's become too much lately and I'm concerned my property value is decreasing. What can I do to keep these people from trashing my place? SWAMPED IN LOS ANGELES.

Dear Swamped: Tell the D.A's Office that although most of the evidence has already been taken from the condo next door, you know of new evidence — a knife, glove, dirty underwear, three wigs, two hairy shirt buttons and a chain saw, for example, in the basement of a house in the ghetto. *(Scout it out first. It should be vacant and look haunted for a future movie site)*. This false information, of course, will leak to the media and film-makers, so the attention will be diverted elsewhere. If this ruse fails, contact your Neighborhood Watch commander and tax accountant to determine if tickets and T-shirt sales are a community service and therefore tax deductible.

Dear Gary: I'm concerned by polls showing my popularity is deteriorating daily. I've tried my best to do what's right, but nothing I do seems to help. What do you think the problem is, and what should I do? TRAPPED IN A WHITE HOUSE.

Dear Trapped: The problem is you campaigned on a Big Mac platform, but put sloppy joes on the table. Where's the beef? That's what the people want to know. You tried for a fat-free health program, but all it had was pork. Your foreign policy is still foreign to any intelligent observer; and, let's be honest, only in your mind were you prepared for this job that nobody could handle properly anyway. Quit this week and accompany *Lonely in Haiti* on his early retirement adventures.

Dear Gary: I'm bored counting my millions of dollars and playing golf. I've learned money isn't everything. What can I do to get back on the baseball field and play again? STRIKER ONE.

Dear Striker: Repentance is good, so is money. Play the field. Call Pete Rose. Play basketball, football, soccer, boxing and the ponies. Good luck!

———————

The best advice is your own. Take it.

Beating the IRS Takes Guts and a Little Sickness

The *good* news is I won't be doing time splitting rocks, and Dianna, my former accountant, has found gainful work doing landscape gardening in the Everglades.

The *bad* news is the IRS didn't agree that incorporating my family and writing off expenses for food, clothing, transportation, gifts, vacations and unusual psychiatric care were legitimate or legal.

Last year, if you recall, I decided families should be treated as small businesses and be given appropriate tax deductions as an incentive to stay together. The government, after all, says the deterioration of America is due to the nuclear family going ballistic. Unfortunately, after I filed for a $25,000 tax refund based on my $20,000 income, I received an IRS mail-bomb: *"Please be advised your tax return reflects serious anomolies, inconsistencies, inappropriate filing forms, questionable charitable contributions and you didn't sign where indicated."*

Something was wrong! *"Please prepare a pot of strong coffee, your receipts and notify your next of kin."* An auditor was coming!

I called a tax attorney, explaining my predicament. He coughed loudly and excused himself from further conversation. I couldn't reach Dianna — she was swamped with work in Florida. My father-in-law had conveniently gone on a Las Vegas vacation. I had to tough it out alone.

"Come on in, the coffee is ready Mr. Smith," I said with my best fake charm. "How's your wife and kids?"

"I don't drink coffee. I'm a single, gay, minority bachelor with an attitude, and I don't like you already," he said. He reminded me of Carrie, a high-school date I didn't get along with, who was later jailed for killing a Grizzly bear with her bare hands.

"Okay. Well, here are the receipts. I've got them organized by date, amount and category."

"That won't do. They need to be on a CD ROM."

"What?"

"The new paperless system. If you don't comply there will be penalties and interest payments on what you owe."

"Who said I owe? You haven't even audited yet!"

"Don't need to. You look guilty. It's obvious. Your eyelids are quivering. How could you afford that Mercedes in the driveway? Where did you get this leather sofa? How can you maintain the upkeep on the Siamese cat and French poodle?"

"Give me a break! The car was given to us by a friend who borrowed $1,000 from us. He invested in commodities or something and made a killing, so he shared his good fortune. My wife and I got the sofa at a midnight garage sale. We didn't know it was leather until we woke up in the morning after the party and discovered it was easy to clean. We adopted the cat and dog from the kennel because we wanted some extra deductions for dependents. See, here are the receipts for the food and medical care . . . and then . . ."

"I see here you deducted $6,000 for depreciation on a hotel on Marvin Gardens and $20,000 for investments in three motels on Park Place. You a friend of Donald Trump?"

"Not exactly. We were playing Monopoly with Fred and Martha and signed IOUs. We take our game very seriously."

"What's this five hundred bucks here for charitable contributions to the local government?"

"We're real proud of that. We gave that money to a burglar. He promised he would leave the neighborhood and let us keep our VCR and video camera if we taped him escaping and let the local news station play it. We figured we saved a few thousand in law enforcement expenses, while helping him re-gain his self esteem."

"Uh, huh. Interesting. What's this $2,000 deduction for 'special medical expenses' ?"

"Well, Mr. Smith, that's kinda personal. Every April 15th my wife and I get kinda edgy with the pressure and all, so we take a vacation after dropping off our return at the airport post office."

"Huh?"

"We have to see a special doctor in the Bahamas for our allergy. If we're not treated immediately we become irrationally violent and do things we're not proud of."

"What kind of allergy requires a trip to the Bahamas?"

"Tax allergy. If we feel we might have to pay we shred all our records and threaten to go on a hunger strike unless we can deduct our food and medical expenses."

"Who's the doctor?"

"Sometimes it's Dr. Ruth and sometimes it's Dr. Kevorkian. It depends on how our audits turn out each year."

"I'm outa here!"

Vacation Plan Saves Ancient Travel Agent From Ruin

My travel agent Herbert Hipple greeted me with a yawn. The famous traveler and author of *Tripping On $hoestrings*, now 79, still lives covertly in his cabin by the river.

"How's it going, Herbie?" I asked. "Nice to see you again."

"Yeah, yeah, yeah."

"Why are you so crabby?"

"Technology has passed me by. Can't compete with the agencies anymore. Hate computers. Can't just pick up the phone anymore. Can't just make deals with my persuasive voice. Besides, I'm gettin' too old for this work. It's all over. Time to fish."

"Maybe my timing is bad, Herbie, but we're *really* broke this time. I promised my family an exciting summer adventure and . . ."

"I know. You want a freighter to Africa or cargo plane to South America. Can't do it. Don't know how to use the Internet. Don't wanna even try."

"Well, Herbie, I wish you could come up with something exciting for us that's unusual and inexpensive. You know us so well after these twenty-two years."

"That, I do!"

"C'mon, Herbie."

"Well, okay — give me a few days."

Several days later. "Okay, I've got something *very* special for you. Talked to some of my friends who still use the phone."

Herbie, using his wall map, began the tour.

"I've arranged with my friend Jimmy for you to test drive a GM experimental electric car. He's an engineering consultant for the company. Helped him climb Mt. Everest a couple years ago. When you arrive in Bismarck, you'll meet Willie. He'll give you his 30-foot barge. I figure you'll get to St. Louis in a month with favorable currents down the Missouri. Saved his life just recently — pulled his parachute open on a recent sky-dive trip.

"In St. Louis you'll tie up with Reggie. He and I once owned the *Mississippi Princess*. He's arranged free passage on the old lady. She leaks a little, but the paddles can still get the steamer down river in good time. In two weeks you'll get to New Orleans and meet Maggie, my seventh wife, who still collects alimony from me and owns a shrimp trawler. She'll take you on the scenic route to Miami where my scuba buddy from the Navy Seals, Johnny, will take you to Cuba in his four-man sub.

"Then you'll roller blade to Guantanamo Bay with Jose. I once helped him develop a self-adhesive cigar wrapper. He's doin' well in the skate business, too, I hear. Now you'll board a military transport headed for Hawaii. General MacInsock will join you. I've kept quiet for years about our little golf outing to the Virgin Islands on a B-52 bomber."

"Isn't this the long route? Why not book us on a freighter directly to Hawaii?"

"Hang on a minute, buddy. I tried. My pal Reggie is still in jail. Stowed away with a young lady client of mine after I arranged her legitimate voyage. He's tyin' the knot with her when he gets out. He owes me one for fixin' him up.

"When you reach Maui, Wana Bewanna will take your family to an isolated rock cave on the beach, inaccessible by car, train, plane or helicopter."

"How are we going to get there?"

"Bike. Wana worked with me in the CIA travel agency and was also an undercover Olympic bicyclist. The cave has recently been remodeled. Even has a barbecue pit. You'll enjoy a few days of rest and spiritual rejuvenation. Then Wana will return to guide you through the jungle back to the airport."

"Jungle?"

"He's going to video-tape your adventure for his bicycle commercial. Never did much for him at the CIA, but obviously can't talk about that. Then it's back home on a 50-foot sailboat, my compliments. Third wife got it — makes the trip six times a year for me — part of the divorce settlement."

"Wow, Herbie. You've really done it this time. How much will all this cost?

"Not much. All I want from you is an account of your adventure to promote my new book, *Travel-Lite*. And I want to borrow your computer. Maybe I can make a few extra nickels tapping into this new-fangled gadgetry after all. It's worth a try, isn't it?"

"No, Herbie. You're amazing with the phone. Stick with it."

My vacation request had given Herbie new life and the inspiration to go on. That was payment enough, I thought, after telling him we decided this was more adventure than we could handle. I suggested he take his plan to Hollywood for a movie.

I hope he listened, although it'll be tough replacing him. A travel agent with his imagination and telephone skills could make more than a few nickels in Fantasyland.

Another Can of Worms for Tax Time

I'm glad Dianna, my tax accountant, is back. She always did look forward to our annual April challenge. Apparently, she lost her job in the Everglades doing floral landscaping — certainly not as exciting as doing taxes for vagrants like me.

Now she gets to hear about my ingenious tax-saving scams and collect her ridiculous fee for filling out all those important-looking documents to impress the IRS.

When I went to her office and opened up this year's can of worms, things were pretty messy.

"Get those slimy things off my desk," she shrieked. "You're nuts!" Dianna is usually right about *some* things.

"I hear the boys and girls in Washington are passing new tax laws to help the poor, so I'm getting an early start in my new business venture this year."

"Oh no, not again. What is it this time?"

"A worm farm. Don't you remember how we incorporated my family and deducted food, clothing, vacations and lawn care as business expenses? Remember the fun we had with the auditor? He got so flustered over my psychiatric medical deductions that I had to recommend some of my shrinks to him?

"Well, after he said home improvements were legit deductions, I landscaped the entire yard. Turned that weed patch into a genuine rock and plant paradise. That's when I discovered this whole society of helpless underground critters. They were just squirming around hiding from the birds. Now I'm hoping they'll prefer dancing in fresh water to entertain the fish."

"But Gary, why a worm farm?"

"I figure I can make a bundle with these creatures. I want to get a quick start. You know, 'the early bird' . . ."

"Funny. What makes you think you're going to make money?"

"For one, I'll have tons of deductions for dirt removal and replacement. This is a requirement for good worm nutrition, you know. I'm also doing my patriotic duty to support the presidential campaign. I'm buying several expensive, custom-made Dole, Gingrich, Clinton and Buchanan mannequins. They'll make terrific scarecrows to keep those winged scavengers away from my creepy little money-makers."

"You're kidding?"

"Nope. I support free enterprise and the work ethic. It's important to do unto others before they do unto you and . . ."

"Whoa! Let's get back to taxes and forget about the gobbledygook. And get these worms off my desk. I'm getting ill."

"Good. See, Dianna, that's why I can get away with lots of deductions for their care and maintenance. No IRS auditor will want to see up close and personal how I stuff the critters in cans and ship them to fishing stores and gourmet pasta restaurants."

"Oh, God!"

"I'm also taking the $500 child deduction for every ton of worms I raise. Seems fair. I don't have any children, and the auditor didn't allow for my rabbits in the last audit. I'm deducting educational expenses for studying worm life in Kenya, Bora Bora, Argentina and France. It's similar to politicians studying those creepy, human night crawlers in places like Haiti, Somalia and Iraq."

Dianna shook her head, baffled again by my brilliance.

"I'm deducting the cost of producing a series for cable TV's fishing channel. It's to be called *Unearthing the Truth About Worm Fishing*. I'll be shown catching 24-pound bass every time I use one of my two-pound, genetically-engineered worms."

"Geez. I don't know about fishing, but . . . two pounds?"

"Yep. I'll deduct the expense of developing my DNA cross-breeding, gene-splicing process. I call the liquid feeding potion Snake-in-the-Glass. My boa constrictor and that last IRS auditor were important ingredients of my discovery."

"Whew! I can see you've given your new venture a lot of thought," said Dianna. "But did you hear there are new taxes on inventions and career changes?"

"Nope."

"Well, based on your projections, you'll net a profit of $13 for the year. That includes your costs for another audit and tax court visit, psychiatric evaluations, employee health inspections and . . ."

"Employees? How can my flock of trained worm-collecting canaries be inspected? I'm only using six of them as deductions. I even paid their veterinarian health insurance! Here are the receipts."

Dianna's head hit her desk.

Fortunately it missed this year's can of worms.

Romans First To Benefit From Super Bowl

This year's Super Bowl will prove what the playful Romans knew before us. Stadium violence is a sure-fire way to make big bucks on the glorification of human agony. Alcoholic beverages sell well, too, in the name of sport.

Things panned out for the prospecting 49ers, seeking world domination again. And the underdog gladiators from the south, I heard, are getting charged up by recruiting large, hairy animals from the San Diego zoo and Camp Pendleton to fight in the Miami arena.

Celebrity commentators will be Rush and Hillary. O.J. will report from the sidelines. He's been temporarily released from jail so he can earn money to repay Hertz for abusing a rented Ford Bronco and take a break from doing his gig at the courthouse.

Here are excerpts from of the trio's pre-game analyses.

RUSH: "Geez. I can't believe I signed up for this gig, working with a suspected felon and a FemiNazi."

HILLARY: "Shut up Rush, you bloated, arrogant imbecile. You're doing it for the money and your ego, just like me. You know less about football than politics."

RUSH: "Don't talk to me like that, Mrs. Liberal One. You probably took this assignment to raise public support for spending taxpayers' money to hire government referees to stem violence in football, basketball and hockey games."

O.J.: "Knock it off, you two, or I'll do it for you. Don't let violence jeopardize my short probation. Let's keep the commentary strictly on the game."

HILLARY: "Well, I think San Diego will win. The team has recruited well. Its defense is strong and its offense is highly motivated and . . ."

RUSH: "Whoa! Its offense is that Proposition 187 wasn't enforced. I'm investigating to see if all the players have green cards."

HILLARY: "You're nuts!"

O.J.: "Let me take a stab at a prediction. I think San Francisco will rip San Diego apart. If it rains, the 49ers have an added edge. Their receivers are using my newest collectors' item. It's an autographed glove with a secret red, sticky substance. It's selling very well, thank you."

RUSH: "That won't help a bit, O.J., and I'm suspicious of those San Francisco boys. They'll get too distracted in the huddles."

HILLARY: "You're obnoxious. How can you say that after we've proved gays can be warriors in combat?"

RUSH: "Because when I visited the players in the locker room they all stared at me in that funny little way."

O.J.: "Don't flatter yourself Rush. Players always look suspiciously at journalists who sweat *before* asking the dumb questions. But 'Do you think there should be fines for patting butts?'"

RUSH: "Oh. That was stupid. Anyway, I hate to admit it, but I agree with Hillary. I think San Diego will win because its star running back, Natrone Means, has a name befitting a winner."

HILLARY: "There you go again, Rush. Only thinking in your simplistic macho style."

O.J.: "Well, I'm going to be the roving, on-field reporter, so I'll keep you informed of important details like who is scheduled for the 'Hi Mom' shots."

RUSH: "Ha! And how are you going to get around with those shackles and handcuffs on?"

O.J.: "It won't be easy. But I've been given permission to remove the cuffs when serving Florida orange juice to the players and coaches on the sidelines."

RUSH: "How do we know you won't poison some of the key San Diego players?"

O.J.: "Because I get my bonus only if I serve the teams more juice than my quota."

HILLARY: "Well. I must say I'm looking forward to the game. My legal training will help me provide impartial, non-partisan analysis of every play."

RUSH: "And I'll be wearing the oversized, red boxer legal briefs you gave me, Hillary, in the hopes my commentary won't be too conservative or over-expansive."

O.J.: "And I'll use my experience to describe who's getting away with murder at the bottom of the piles."

Hillary: "Bill and I are looking forward to having the winning team come to the White House for dinner."

O.J.: "Wish I could join you, but I'm needed in court."

RUSH: "I'd join you and the team too, Hillary, but I just can't let my fans know I would socialize with those boys from San Francisco or those illegals from San Diego."

HILLARY: "You aren't invited."

The Romans knew violence would draw the crowds and make money. I'm sure they also had entertaining and controversial commentators to stir up the issues of the day.

PART SIX:
Seriously, Folks

What You Want Isn't What You Get

I was young when I learned that what you wanted wasn't necessarily what you got unless your parents lived in old lamps and could grant more than three wishes.

I think of this lesson often as our government wrangles over balancing a budget that can provide everyone with what they want. It's impossible, so what's the use?

My practical parents, who unfortunately weren't genies, explained one day when I was seven, that I could have either the new bicycle or food. I chose the wheels because I wasn't hungry that morning. That evening I disassembled the bike with a hammer and got *most* of it back in the box. My compassionate parents let me eat dinner without giving me any lectures.

Back then, credit cards and bankers didn't make it as easy as now to buy things you didn't really need. Financial restraint is still a problem, and now credit cards and lenders abound to push us along the road to bankruptcy. Ditto for the government. I can simplify the budget concept for our politicians by referring to my personal history.

I didn't get that bicycle until I was nine but had eaten lots of healthy food so I was big enough to ride it. At 11, I wanted my own telephone but learned to write letters instead. At 12, I wanted a fashionable raincoat but got used to an old umbrella. At 13, I wanted to be a warrior with a BB gun, but armed myself with words instead.

At 15, I wanted a set of drums to relieve adolescent tension but just beat up on my kid brother instead. At 16, I wanted a car, but it was easier to bum rides than convince my parents I was worth the expense. At 17, I wanted a huge allowance just for being a teenager but learned welfare wasn't included in the family budget. At 18, I wanted to attend Harvard Law School. I wasn't able to understand the rules for filling out the application forms, so I went to junior college instead to learn how.

At 21, I wanted to dodge the Draft but it was blowing in the wrong direction. Reluctantly I served my country for meager wages and learned that self-discipline is easier when enforced by tough bosses. At 23, I wanted a high-paying executive position as a reward for graduating college but settled for just a job. At 25, I wanted a substantial pay raise for doing average work but accepted the humor of my employer's sympathy card. And then, at 26, I wanted a new job with more difficult challenges but instead got stuck at the same old job with a large pay increase for exceptional work.

At 27, I wanted a new car but remembered my parents' admonition and settled again for food. At 35, I wanted to buy a big house with a swimming pool and tennis court but had to buy a small one with running water and a Ping-Pong table.

Many of the things I wanted I never got. But I got what I needed. I once had a new Volkswagen. I traveled to Europe. I enjoyed the good bread and cheese, although sleeping in vineyards wasn't comfortable when it rained. I once had fashionable clothes, even though I couldn't wear them often because I couldn't afford dry cleaning. I got a fishing boat, although inflating it got me out of breath, so I didn't use it much either. And finally, I got a computer that corrects my spelling, but it's kinda old and makes miss steaks.

I'm afraid I've been a big disappointment to lenders who have encouraged me to borrow their money for things I didn't need. I've enjoyed the use of many credit cards because it's a kick paying off the bills before owing any interest money. I've borrowed to buy a house because it's patriotic to own a mortgage. And I've borrowed for investments — once to get into a high-stakes poker game in Texas with drunk players I could bluff and once to pay taxes I then conveniently forgot to pay. After all, some necessities are too important to ignore!

I wish our government would stop playing political games with our money and be responsible — pay for what we need, *not* what we want. It's painful. It doesn't get votes.

But the natural laws of responsibility must apply to our trusted politicians as well as to individual citizens.

It would be a lot easier if we could find a friendly genie.

Hearing Doesn't Help People Listen

"Where are my purple-striped pants?" I hollered at my wife.

When she told me she threw them away so I wouldn't embarrass her anymore in front of her friends, I was angry. But she just smiled. No anger. No argument. No stress. I had recently given her some ear plugs for these occasions. She put them in quickly.

I, too, became silent.

She walked over to me and whispered in my ear, "I love you when you say nothing."

I owe the success of my experiment to Everett Richardson. He had written in to share important news. At 71, he had obviously learned to filter out the unpleasant sounds of ideas he doesn't like. He couldn't hear his wife suggest he needed a hearing aid.

He refused to pay the $50 to have his ears cleaned just so the salesman could provide the free hearing test advertised in the paper. Mr. Richardson could see no benefit from spending another $300 to purchase the chic, high-tech hearing device. He prefers buying food for the pigeons and seagulls at the State Park beach.

He swears he can still hear the ripples of meager waves softly caressing the sand and gravel on shore between midnight and six a.m. "when kids aren't using those damned boom boxes."

He explained his condition: he can hear fine, "but I just don't understand the way I used to."

His pursuit of a CB hobby conflicts with his otherwise logical frame of mind. As a CB radio buff, he knows that "everybody's talking, nobody's listening, and it doesn't matter because what's being said isn't worth listening to anyway." Obviously, he's a masochist with a sense of humor. He doesn't understand himself like he used to because he can't hear himself think and probably doesn't want to.

Mr. Richardson isn't alone. He's got my vote as a future City Council member. His wisdom would be a welcome addition to solving our city's financial problems. He could balance the budget logically, and he wouldn't be swayed by the emotional bickering of special interest groups and political insiders because he couldn't hear them.

He'd probably make a fine Speaker of the House in Washington, D.C. He could smile and nod enthusiastically at the blow-hard members of Congress he didn't care to listen to, and *read* carefully the arguments of substance for funding studies on the environmental impact of seagulls' and pigeons' appetites or supporting two-month term limits for elected officials who talk more than listen. *(The Honorable Mr. Richardson would speak only after he figured out who they were).*

Aside from the obvious political advantages of Mr. Richardson's condition, his disability would also be an asset as a rock concert critic. Nobody can hear the words to the music anyway; he could concentrate on critiquing the artistic body movements and antics of the performers or the special effects or the reaction of the crowd. That's really what determines the success or failure of most musical events anyway.

He wrote that his condition did have a downside. It had seriously damaged his beloved wife's tolerance — until he purchased a TV remote control. "I had to ask her to turn up the volume after she had turned it down during commercials. That was too much exercise for her, getting up and down. But now she can relax. I can adjust the volume to hear the gunfights and car chases and turn it down when irritated victims on talk shows yell and scream at each other."

I've learned much from Mr. Richardson's letter. I listened intently to the meaning of the words in my mind as clearly as he typed them on paper. "I hear fine," he said, "it's just that the sounds I hear don't compute like they used to."

I understand what Mr. Richardson said in closing his letter.

"I'd hate to give up the peaceful silence," he wrote. "In today's noisy world, being hard of hearing may be a blessing."

My wife agreed — and kept the ear plugs.

Solid Friendships Don't Follow the Wind

It's no secret a living friend is the most precious commodity in the world, unless you're a greedy tycoon and prefer profits from pork bellies and soy bean futures.

Most friendships historically go the way of fair winds: when it's warm and gentle, look for good times; when it's windy and cold, good luck finding any comfort.

There are exceptions.

It's Dave's 50th birthday. I searched despairingly for the appropriate gift to pay tribute to our 30-year friendship. I couldn't afford the red Ferrari he's always wanted, but remembered the adage, *It's the thought that counts*. I feel better now.

Instead, I've decided to "roast" him. This will be his gift.

We met in 1967 in the worst of circumstances. We were drafted into the Army, imprisoned at Fort Hood, Texas. His quiet demeanor kept him out of trouble. My boisterous, rebellious personality kept me on the verge of lock-ups in the brig or, worse yet, 30 consecutive days of KP.

During those two years, Dave's quiet wisdom and advice stopped me from telling off bully sergeants and cocky officers. He always had the right words to explain why my behavior wasn't appropriate for such an organization. I responded in kind when he stabbed himself in the hand with a bayonet while standing at attention in a parade. This single act abruptly erased any hope that he could protect me in a combat situation.

He taught me to how race my 1956 Chevy, *The Green Latrine*, down Texas highways, and I reciprocated by making him pay the tickets. He taught me to fake illness to escape KP, and I taught him to earn money by lending it at 50 percent.

After surviving The Battle of Texas, our friendship developed into a more practical relationship in accordance with our means. We shared a one-room apartment in Los Angeles where we learned that barbecued chuck roasts tasted better than prime rib and that buying new plastic dishes was better than washing dirty, old ceramic ones that broke when you dropped them.

We shared illusions about improving our status. "I'm going to be a CBS anchorman when Cronkite retires," I said; and he said, with his knowing smile, "And I'll watch you every night."

During college, Dave rescued me from failure several times, convincing me to edit eloquent sentences from my term papers nobody would understand like, *And the War of 1812 proved once again that without historical adversity, songwriters and composers couldn't make a living today.*

Dave was always there. He laughed when the doctor ripped out my tonsils and I was unable to talk for the second time in my life. The first was after eating chipped beef and cream sauce in the Army.

He supported me when I graduated and couldn't find a job. He married Diann. They welcomed me into their apartment as an older-type orphan dependent and then when I found a job, gracefully kicked me out with kind words: "We've enjoyed having you stay with us. We'll enjoy seeing you again later. Much later."

He helped me bury my mother when others were too busy. He tolerated my paranoia, neuroses, impulsive behavior and incessant talking, admitting years later he never paid much attention anyway.

He convinced me many times that the world wasn't ending that day but I could take my time and worry for the whole week if I chose.

He conned me into selling my car so I could return to Italy, where I had met the woman who would become my first wife. I thought at first he did this to get me out of his hair; but I realized later when he stood as my best man, that he really was a best man.

Someone said if you have health you have everything. If, however, he hadn't been there when I was wheeled in for two heart surgeries and been there when I awoke, I'm not sure the outcome would have mattered as much.

Along with my wife and my dog, Dave is the best friend I've ever known. His wife, Diann, is in the same category.

Dave is interesting. I've called him boring, in jest, of course, because his quiet demeanor conceals his many passions. But his actions are loud and clear. This book wouldn't exist without him.

His tolerance, intelligence, sick sense of humor, patience and lack of business acumen, are the good reasons I hired him to be my unpaid editor and partner.

Happy birthday, Dave. Your friendship is a rock.

Children Teach If You're Willing To Listen

The post-season pizza party was a sad occasion.

I said good-bye to members of my 2nd-grade Boys and Girls Club basketball team. The short season was over. I was fortunate to have been their coach.

I learned more about teamwork from watching them improve on their own, than they learned from my continuous stream of "do this and do that" rhetoric.

When the season started the kids could barely throw the ball high enough to reach the basket. Tying their shoes and keeping their shorts on were equally difficult obstacles to their peak performances.

Kyle and Matt were reminders of my own early childhood. They, too, were left out of the action. They thought dribbling was something they did well when they slept.

Kyle couldn't pass the ball with any authority or accuracy, hitting teammates in the back instead of the hands. Matt seemed to know something no one else did. He watched the action around him as he stood still with a great big smile, doing nothing.

Tony, a defensive genius, swarmed opponents like an angry bee but couldn't distinguish basketball from football, running like a halfback without bouncing the ball.

David could dribble — oh, could he dribble. He dribbled here, there and everywhere — until the other team ganged up on him — and then he threw the ball off the court or got it stolen. And there was Caleb. A grin on his face said with confidence, "just wait, coach, just wait," as he dropped the ball, passed it off the court and threw it at the basket like a Michael Jordan commercial — nothing but air.

Michael was so small I wondered how he would feel playing with Aaron and Jimmy, our tall and powerful *franchise* players. But Michael dribbled so well and ran so fast, he weaved his way around everyone and could steal the ball easily because few seemed capable of finding him.

"No, no, David," I yelled. "Pass the ball, don't dribble. Aaron, don't take those long shots. You're *not* Michael Jordan!" I screamed. "Kyle, Matt, are you going to play or do you want to sit and watch? Tony, let go of his leg!"

We had drills and more drills. My encouraging voice echoed off the gymnasium walls heard little by the players doing their own kind of prodding: "I'm open, Caleb, throw it." "Kyle, I'm open." "Jimmy, I'm open." "Tony, throw it here." "Matt, I'm open."

And they would throw it. Again and again and again. Most of the time to the other team or to frustrated parents watching on the sidelines. It didn't matter. They were having fun.

That was eight weeks ago.

"Okay, you guys. This is our last game, then it's pizza."

"Yea," they said in unison.

"Any questions?" I asked.

"Tell everyone to stop yelling and telling us what to do. It makes me nervous," said David.

"Okay. Who hasn't made a basket this season?" Kyle and Michael shyly raised their hands.

"What are we going to do about that?"

The whistle blew.

Michael took the ball, ran like a rabbit across the entire floor and made his first basket of the year! It was a sight to behold!

Kyle dribbled slowly, very slowly, then threw a spectacular one-bounce pass hard at the feet of Aaron, who took the ball to the hoop and scored. Then Caleb stole the ball, dribbled down court, and watched hopefully as his lay-up rimmed the hoop and almost went in. He was becoming a player. It was in his eyes. It was intense.

Excitement filled the air. Time out.

"Okay boys, do you want to win or have fun?" I asked. "Have fun," they said unanimously, knowing that's what I preached, though not what they believed.

"Lets do it, then."

Tony alertly stole the ball, passed to Aaron who passed to Jimmy who made the basket. Then Matt knocked the ball loose from the opponent, David picked it up, dribbled adroitly and passed to Aaron who ran the length of the court and was wide open for an easy lay-up. But he didn't shoot!

He gave it to Kyle. Kyle shot, missed. Aaron got the rebound again, but didn't shoot the easy hoop. He passed to Kyle. Kyle shot and missed. Jimmy got the rebound and passed to Kyle. He shot and missed again. The referee blew the whistle. "Foul. Two shots."

Kyle went to the free-throw line. Two minutes left. He missed the first. A miracle — his second shot was perfect! The crowd roared. Kyle turned around, faced his fans and grinned the biggest grin I had ever seen. It was beautiful.

Life was good. Kyle was a player!

"Why didn't you shoot when you were open?" I asked Jimmy and Aaron after the game.

"We wanted Kyle to make a basket and be happy."
Their unselfish act made the season worthwhile. I wept.

As I drove to the pizza party, I reflected on the game and knew that coaching is giving kids confidence to improve on their own, with simple guidelines and little intrusion.

I wish everyone could have seen the White Tornadoes, their courage and teamwork and the big grins that went along with their athletic growth and wisdom.

Those were some of my life's greatest moments.

Sex and Violence Are Natural Laws To Be Obeyed

Attacking the entertainment industry for exploiting violence and sex is a frightening excuse for poor leadership.

Politicians are again searching for convenient scapegoats to blame for our deteriorating moral substance. I rarely write serious stuff because I prefer using humor to soften my cynical attitudes about society. But even irreverent humor should not be subjected to government influence, which is seriously offensive.

There is only one significant correlation between our deteriorating society and the entertainment industry. A film, a recording and a society, each has its own life, death and hopefully, a rebirth. Each plants roots in history to later be regenerated — it's part of the eco-(nomic) system.

The so-called immoral bias of the entertainment industry is merely a reflection of Uncle Sam's age and soul. Maybe he's suffering from maturity.

I agree with the would-be censors only in one area. We must have a system which prevents youngsters from exposure to the dirty linen of our moral fabric.

Sex and violence have been around a long time. In a perfect world they always will be. It's nature.

222

The *Leave It To Beaver* mentality is fine. It's a positive influence. But the concept is as unrealistic today as it was then. We're all too busy. Women don't wear aprons and smile all day. Men can't be expected to leave their remote controls to put on coats and ties and negotiate during family feuds.

In contrast, I also accept the *Natural Born Killers* mentality. It's bad, but the success of that movie clearly illustrates our interest in evil, insane, and fascinating miscreants. The movie provides a visual and educational depiction of the totally natural inclination of a deviant to pursue what he or she is supposed to do.

The images of violence and evil, not legislation or verbal bashing, stimulate the pursuit of virtuous values like love and beauty.

It's yin and yang.

Those in government who think of blocking violent or sexually stimulating adventures in films, books or music, should remember that Bible movies like the *Ten Commandments* and *Spartacus* introduced the public to mass murder in the name of God. Let them not forget their endorsements of heroism in WWII movies depicting the massacres of thousands. Evil can provoke good, and good often provides an opportunity for evil — we all have some of both in us, admittedly or not.

Perhaps Washington would like to start up its own movie studio. Hitler did. Then we might see classics like *Washington Whispers*, the true story about the deft CIA censors who quietly save America by assassinating traitors like Clint Eastwood, Sylvester Stallone, Arnold Schwarzenneger, Oliver Stone and anyone else exploiting for profit the realities of violence and sexuality — classic hypocrisy in our world of ironies.

A government studio couldn't profit from politically-motivated propaganda films of scripted Rose Garden speeches and one-sided press conferences. Who would want to watch *Mr. Rogers Dances On Sesame Street* or *Tea With Miss Manners*? Would we watch Arnold in *The Terminator*, if he were being attacked by bees while picking weeds instead of eliminating bad guys?

The politicians screaming for restraint in films and music, I'm afraid, are looking to trade scapegoats for election votes. Before raising more curtains on the censorship issue, they should clean up their *own* acts which would expose their own lack of leadership and deteriorating ethical and moral values.

If Washington wishes to continue its assault on the entertainment industry, it should first entertain the reality that much evil comes from within its own house. Viet Nam killed people; Watergate destroyed confidence in our government; political fraud harms legitimate businesses and the working man. The list is long.

And Hollywood loves doing what it's supposed to do — make money from unusual and compelling stories. Hollywood produces entertainment for profit. Movie-goers obviously like violence and sex. They are laws of nature. They must be obeyed. The exploitation provides a respite from the humdrum of normal lives. It may cost too much to produce and see these reality-based fantasies, but it's a lot healthier for a free society than force-fed, tax-funded movies any Washington studio would encourage us to see.

We have choices. I enjoyed *Casper* as much as *Patton*. I loved *Beaver* but found *Killers* exciting as well as educational. But you won't see me haunting your house, guiding armies to victory, yelling "Hey, Wally" in the streets or shooting people with a shotgun, just because I saw the movies.

When I can't write what I think, and you can't read what I write, then the deterioration of our society will be complete.

I hope that's not a scene from a future classic any of us would want our descendants to see.

Simplicity, Innocence: Keys to Life and Death

My best friend has died.

Humor has served well to shield me and others from pain and to make serious issues funny so I survive each day with some sanity.

But things are different this week. I feel no humor, only sadness, but I'm wiser now — and better.

The terror and anguish of abandonment have finally been erased from my soul. My father died and left me when I was 13. He acted tough to protect me, but sadly was too weak to say good-bye. So I, too, acted tough. I had to be strong for my mother and younger siblings. I never cried. I know now neither my father nor I were really very tough at all.

I held my friend tightly in my arms, inhaling his wonderful, familiar smell, and stroked his silky, golden hair for the last time. I cried uncontrollably as I thanked him for 15 years of love and asked forgiveness for the moments I was unkind. I whispered in his ear, "I love you, Bear," and felt the last breath escape from his body when the doctor injected the fatal chemical.

His beautiful, peaceful face made me feel both relief and loss. But I didn't feel abandoned this time. I got to say good-bye. He had a great, long life and a peaceful death. He shared both with me. My father didn't. And now I'm finally able to release the anger I've embraced for so long.

I'm stronger now. With Bear I was able to experience life's full spectrum — beginning, middle and end. I'm more in touch with what's important. Today I was fully able to appreciate the pleasure the little girl next door had as she picked a flower and tossed it into the wind with a smile. Simplicity and innocence. That's what's important and real in life and in death.

These traits were apparent every day of Bear's life and in the moment of his death. His purity provided both of us with some wonderful pleasures. Trust, beauty, joy, companionship, love, patience, curiosity and tolerance were all there. There were no strings attached. His life was simple, pure and beautiful.

I remember him years ago chasing a rabbit he could never catch and getting lost in a ravine. Wet, exhausted and frightened, he never left my side again. I think of him catching his favorite tennis ball in the air, running and then dropping it at my feet for another game of catch, until I was exhausted.

He was a clever fellow. He designed his own obstacle course in the yard, leaping over, under and through bushes in the same pattern every time, giving plenty of hind-leg salutes to his favorite trees along the way. He was also a bit too innocent at times, approaching every cat with a friendly wag of his tail, only to be rejected with an unexpected hiss.

He had good manners, wiping his face clean on the carpet after every meal. He showed pride, pointing out with his nose and outstretched tail any animal climbing a tree, and revealed shame, lowering his head after he relieved himself in the house when I selfishly forgot about him. He displayed patience and love, nudging my hand for a moment of affection or curling up so naturally next to me with his head on my lap. He instinctively knew when I was in a bad mood and accepted the rejection without question.

He buried objects of value, like bones and my shoes, and joyfully chased fresh air, snowflakes, and birds, for pleasures I've never understood. He tolerated my temper tantrums and questionable music from the piano I play and watched curiously as I threw computer paper in the air and cursed when I couldn't think of anything good to write on too many occasions.

Most of all, he was just there. Always. He was a miracle. I never wanted to believe Bear would leave me as my father did, but knew one day he would. That day has come and gone. With new wisdom I can now live out my own years, appreciating my own innocence and simplicity, without questioning my existence.

I love Bear like the father I miss. With his departure, I'm now able to understand and pass along what he taught me. That alone, is worth living for.

I'm hoping he's playfully chasing rabbits he'll never catch, romping with other dogs and making friends with many friendly cats.

I miss him so incredibly much.

I hope he has a moment once in awhile, to remember me with the same love I have for him. I'd like that a lot.

God bless you Bear.

Humor me!   BUY MORE BOOKS!

For more copies of ADVENTURES in the SLOW LANE,
please send a check or money order made out to:

**Hardshell Publishing
P.O. Box 1630
Mukilteo, WA 98275**

PUBLISHING

ORDER FORM

Please send___copy(ies) of
ADVENTURES in the SLOW LANE to:

(Name)_____

(Address)_____

(City, State)_____(Zip Code)_____

Enclosed is my check or money order for $11.95 per book,
(*WA State residents add 8.2% sales tax*) plus $2.50 shipping/handling.
(*Please allow two weeks for delivery*)

Indicate if you would like your copy autographed._____

THANK YOU!